THE FIX

How the Twelve Steps Offer a Surprising Path of Transformation for the Well-Adjusted, the Down-and-Out, and Everyone In Between

WORKBOOK

IAN MORGAN CRON

WITH DUDLEY DELFFS

Harper*Christian*
Resources

The Fix Workbook
© 2025 by Ian Morgan Cron

Published in Grand Rapids, Michigan, by HarperChristian Resources. HarperChristian Resources is a registered trademark of HarperCollins Christian Publishing, Inc.

Requests for information should be sent to customercare@harpercollins.com

ISBN 978-0-310-17364-9 (softcover)
ISBN 978-0-310-17365-6 (ebook)

HarperChristian Resources titles may be purchased in bulk for church, business, fundraising, or ministry use. For information, please e-mail ResourceSpecialist@ChurchSource.com.

Ian Morgan Cron is represented by Kathryn Helmers of Helmers Literary Services (helmersliterary.com).

First Printing December 2024 / Printed in the United States of America

CONTENTS

INTRODUCTION

Congratulations! If you're picking up this workbook to maximize the benefit of reading *The Fix*, then you're making a significant investment in your future. If you haven't read my book *The Fix* yet, then I encourage you to read it as you complete the questions and exercises here. While you will benefit from engaging this workbook, it will make more sense and have more personal relevance in tandem with reading the book.

If you're serious about wanting a new way to live, then you're taking a bold step in the right direction. You will discover this workbook is not just a supplement to *The Fix* but also an essential companion for practical application and personal growth. The book explores the Twelve Steps in more detail and illustrates the power they had in the context of my life story when I was facing my addictions. (Yes, that's plural, because just when I think I have a handle on one struggle, another has often seemed to take its place.) Whenever I've reached the end of my rope, the Steps have become my lifeline. This workbook uses that foundation to help you explore and harness the same dynamic power of the Steps in your own life.

You may be thinking, *That's great, Ian. I'm so glad the Steps have helped you and countless alcoholics and addicts . . . but I don't really have a problem with drinking and drugs. So this workbook probably isn't for me.* While I appreciate your concern, let me assure you that the Steps are not just for those who hit rock bottom and find themselves forced into recovery. Addiction takes many forms, and if you're honest, you likely already know that you often rely on certain compulsive patterns more than you should.

This is why it's important to reconsider what you know, or think you know, about the Twelve Steps. They don't just help you abstain from a substance or habitual self-defeating behavior, *though that's obviously a big benefit*. More importantly, they also address the underlying emotional, spiritual, and psychological issues that caused your addiction in the first place. They offer a concise course in expansive living—a different way to relate to yourself, to others, and to God.

The Steps teach you a healthier paradigm for pain management. They teach you how to live joyfully in a broken world where you will never feel quite at home.

What Bill W. and Bob S., the founders of Alcoholics Anonymous and co-authors of the Twelve Steps, recognized almost a hundred years ago still holds true today: *Addiction is principally a spiritual problem — not moral or psychological — that requires a spiritual solution.* The purpose of the Steps, therefore, is to enable anyone, not just alcoholics, to experience a better life by focusing on that spiritual solution. So whether you're currently in crisis mode or have been working the Steps for years, they provide a timeless scaffold for building a better life. Engaged with an open mind and willing heart, they can help you break free from your ongoing addictions, faulty thinking, and default defenses.

Rather than a quick fix or one-and-done solution (which simply don't exist), the Steps invite you to continue your spiritual journey, meeting you wherever you are no matter who you are or what you believe or don't believe. They offer relief, perspective, freedom, joy, and peace to anyone who is "sick and tired of being sick and tired." They are for people who want to stop doing whatever they are doing to make themselves feel better—things that eventually do them more harm than good.

So if you're serious about healing and wholeness, and if you're weary from the crushing weight of addiction or compulsive self-limiting behaviors, then it's time to reconsider the Twelve Steps. If you want the "more" you know is out there, and if you want to enjoy the present instead of reliving the past or worrying about the future, then you're in the right place.

If you want to experience freedom to love—yourself, others, and a power greater than yourself—then pat yourself on the back. Whether you're in recovery for alcohol, drugs, porn, gambling, food, or some other addiction, or you simply want to live beyond a persistent habit impeding your path, the Twelve Steps can move you forward. Their wisdom is yours for the taking.

So take a deep breath, hold it, slowly exhale, and then get ready to step into the life you were meant to live.

— IAN CRON

HOW TO USE THIS WORKBOOK

My hope is that this workbook provides fresh insight, additional info, and spiritual inspiration as you engage with each of the Twelve Steps. While each Step meets you where you are, each one also asks you for honesty, vulnerability, and a willingness to risk. It won't be easy, but it will be rewarding as you acknowledge what's true, what's false, and what's required to move forward.

The apostle Paul compares this kind of growth to changing clothes, removing old garments and putting on new ones that fit better for who you are becoming (see Ephesians 4:22–24). In order to grow and experience the benefits of the Steps, you're invited to examine the recurrent thoughts, false assumptions, and habitual behaviors that keep you stuck. This process allows you to see yourself, your life, and others with new clarity as well as a spiritual perspective. As you understand and let go of why you do what you do, you make room for new patterns, truthful thoughts, and healthy practices.

Toward this goal, each session begins with a story, example, or anecdote to lead you into the heart of its particular Step. From there, you will focus on identifying, removing, and anticipating barriers to growth in "Meeting You Where You Are." This section helps you see how each Step applies to you and your story.

You will then shift to "Moving Forward" by embracing and applying each Step to your experience and where you are at present. This section invites you to consider not only what's been holding you back but also what you need to grow, to heal, and to experience wholeness. While this section is designed for you to complete on your own, you are also encouraged to think about what takeaways you want to share with your group, meeting, or support team.

Finally, each session concludes by "Connecting with Others." These questions and exercises are intended for group discussion, either with others who are also reading *The Fix* and completing this workbook or with trusted individuals in your life such as sponsors and friends and family. The Twelve Steps emphasize the essential role of relationships and community, so even if you're completing this workbook on your own, you're encouraged to share what you're learning and practicing with others who can support and encourage you.

THE TWELVE STEPS

This amended version of the Twelve Steps omits the word *alcohol* in the first Step so you can insert your own addictive substance or nagging behavior of choice.

1. We admitted we were powerless over _____—that our lives had become unmanageable.

2. Came to believe that a Power greater than ourselves could restore us to sanity.

3. Made a decision to turn our will and our lives over to the care of God as we understood Him.

4. Made a searching and fearless moral inventory of ourselves.

5. Admitted to God, to ourselves, and to another human being the exact nature of our wrongs.

6. Were entirely ready to have God remove all these defects of character.

7. Humbly asked Him to remove our shortcomings.

8. Made a list of all persons we had harmed, and became willing to make amends to them all.

9. Made direct amends to such people wherever possible, except when to do so would injure them or others.

10. Continued to take personal inventory and when we were wrong promptly admitted it.

11. Sought through prayer and meditation to improve our conscious contact with God as we understood Him, praying only for knowledge of His will for us and the power to carry that out.

12. Having had a spiritual awakening as the result of these Steps, we tried to carry this message to [our fellow sufferers], and to practice these principles in all our affairs.

1

ADMIT THE TRUTH

**STEP ONE: We admitted we were powerless over
_____ — that our lives had become unmanageable.**

I've been where you are, and I wish I could say Step One is easy.

But it's not. Unless you had extraordinary parents and early caregivers who taught you the art of truth-telling, especially regarding things you are powerless to change, then this first Step may seem like more of a cliff than a curb. It all depends on how far you are from the truth.

If you're brutally honest with yourself, you probably know that willpower—no matter how strong yours might be—is not enough to overcome your sticky attachments. I've always prided myself on pushing through whatever obstacles life throws at me and refusing to quit. Only, some of my ways of coping with acute loss, pain, and crisis persisted and became a way of handling the chronic discomfort, anxiety, and stress of daily living. Thus, an addiction was born, and it grew until I realized what a thief it had become.

No one likes to admit they're defeated—even when you know that you are. We've been conditioned since birth to push through, keep going, fake it 'til you make it, and never let 'em see you sweat. Admitting defeat and accepting that you're powerless is for losers, right? But consider this: How much more do you have to lose before you face the truth?

Step One flies in the face of pretending to be a superhero with a blunt, Kryptonite-studded counterintuitive directive: Admit that you're powerless over your addictions—and, as a result, your life is unmanageable. *Well, actually, Ian, you might be thinking, I can stop any time I want, thank you very much. I don't really have a problem with* _____. *It's just, well, you know . . ."* Yeah, I know, my friend. I know how to translate the language of denial really well—because I became fluent in it a long time ago.

So, even if you are telling yourself that you can conquer your addiction by yourself, humor me for a moment. Just rip the sticky bandage off and accept that Step One applies to everyone and anyone—*including you*. Why? Because Step One is the only one you must accept 100% in its entirety in order to move on to the Steps that follow. Working the Twelve Steps is an ongoing process, again and again and again, that requires grit, determination, and perseverance. If you're not looking the truth about your addictions squarely in the eye, then you will likely falter at some point and start deceiving yourself again.

Many people who turn to the Twelve Steps do so out of desperation. They have hit the lowest point in their lives and have lost everything—family, home, career, health . . . everything. Finally, they come to the realization that they've got no game. They can't beat their addictions by themselves. They can't just white-knuckle it and bulldoze forward on willpower.

I hope you don't have to reach that point to face the truth.

If this is too much for you right now, that's okay. You can either keep going and allow the reality of this truth to sink in slowly or you can close this workbook, put your copy of *The Fix* on the shelf, and wait until this truth becomes undeniable. But I hope you can acknowledge your own powerlessness and keep going. Because if you're bare naked with the truth, you know you probably would not even consider starting this workbook if some part of you wasn't in pain or feeling confused, ashamed, fearful, frustrated, or weary in your soul. Deep down, you know that despite your best efforts, you can't do what you want to do or stop doing what you don't want to do. This is why admitting the truth is your best starting point.

Admitting the truth of Step One frees you to quit trying to change by yourself in your own power. The fundamental truth of this first Step is not that you are weak and defeated but that you need God, you need help from other people, and you need to focus on the reality of your limits in order to grow spiritually. You need a divinely initiated solution to heal the wounds that are driving your addictions and recurrent self-sabotage.

* When have you started out believing yourself "in control" before becoming "out of control" with a substance or behavior? What occurred to cause the shift?

* What *feelings* rise up within you when you consider that you are powerless over your addictions? Check all that apply (and feel free to add your own):

  ☐ defiance   ☐ denial
  ☐ detachment   ☐ fear
  ☐ resentment   ☐ shame
  ☐ regret/guilt   ☐ relief
  ☐ panic   ☐ hope
  ☐ others:

* What *thoughts* rise up within you when you consider that you are powerless over your addictions? Check all that apply (and feel free to add your own):

  ☐ "The Twelve Steps are too extreme for me and my needs."
  ☐ "I should be able to overcome this myself."
  ☐ "I know Step One applies to me, but I still resist admitting its truth."
  ☐ "When I consider my life, I can't deny that my addictions have power over me."
  ☐ "I'm really an addict and need the Twelve Steps just like others."
  ☐ Others:

- What are some areas of your life that have become more difficult to manage as a result of your addictions? What examples come to mind that illustrate how unmanageable these areas are for you right now?

MEETING YOU WHERE YOU ARE

Look, I get it.

No one wants to feel powerless.

No one wants to admit their life is unmanageable.

Powerlessness often takes us back to childhood and times in our lives when we had little to no agency and were unable to stop others from hurting us, leaving us, or shaming us. Those feelings of abandonment and deep sadness, of anger and resentment, of impotence and immobility—no one wants to go through all the ingredients served up by powerlessness.

However, until you admit that you're powerless over your addictions, you will continue to diminish your own power by pretending otherwise. (The irony, right?) The good news implicit in Step One is that you still have plenty of choices. And right now, admitting the truth is one of them.

Step One does not say that you are powerless over your *life*. No, it asserts that you are powerless over your *addictions* and *habitual self-defeating behaviors*. You certainly have the freedom to choose how you respond to many, if not most, aspects of your life on any given day. But your ability to choose also reflects some choices you regret . . . but continue making again and again. Choices about how you handle stress, pain, disappointment, frustration, shame, guilt, trauma, fear, and uncertainty, just to name a few.

If you refuse to admit you're powerless over your addictions, then you give them even more power. If you compulsively keep doing stuff that hurts you and others to numb the pain—then you do not have the power to fix yourself. Because once you start indulging your addictions, denying and ignoring and justifying and sugarcoating them, they take on a power in your life that you didn't realize you were choosing to hand over to them.

The same goes with facing the truth about what's not working in your life. Are you willing to admit the way your addictions consume your life, both internally and externally, with wild abandon? Like a wildfire left unchecked, your addictions will scorch your humanity, inflame your relationships, and incinerate everything you have.

Perhaps at this point you're thinking, *Now, that's a bit overstated, don't you think, Ian? I'm all for hyperbole to make a point, but it's not like I'm some homeless addict trying to pawn his kid's iPad.* Fair enough. But I invite you—no, I dare you—to be honest about what's not working in your life right now as a direct result of your addictions (or, if that word seems too strong, we'll call them "unwanted behaviors" or "addictive patterns"). No matter what label you put on them, you know they're costing you more and more: your peace, your attention, your time, your sanity, your energy, your stability and security. Don't fool yourself that no one else in your life has noticed. Just ask them.

Powerless and *unmanageable* will never be pretty words that you love. Not unless they remove the blindfold of your addictions and allow you to see clearly the truth—and a way forward.

- Describe the last time you felt powerless in the face of an addiction or compulsive behavior. What events, thoughts, and feelings led up to that desire for all that your addiction seemed to offer?

- How have the following areas of your life suffered and become unmanageable because of your relationship with your addictions?

> **Emotional health:** How does coping with the cycle of addiction and its ups and downs take a toll on your moods and feelings most days?

Physical and mental health: What physical ailments, injuries, impairments, and diseases have you suffered as a result (directly or indirectly) of your addictions? How has your mental health been affected by your addictions?

Spiritual health: How has your relationship with God, faith, and spiritual practices changed as a result of your addictions? Why?

Identity and self-worth: How has the way you see yourself changed in light of your ongoing relationship with your addictions? What do you consider the basis for your self-confidence and self-worth?

Relationships with those closest to you: Which relationships have suffered the most or ended as a result of your addictions? Who have you hurt because of your relationship with addictions and compulsive behaviors?

Job and career goals: How has your career and job performance suffered as a result of your addictions? How have your addictions sabotaged your ability to learn, grow, and advance in your field or workplace?

Other areas that have suffered and become unmanageable:

MOVING FORWARD

Admitting the truth usually comes at a cost, and this is true with Step One.

Part of this cost is letting go of your old ways of coping, old ways of deceiving yourself and others, and old ways of delaying your confrontation with the truth. In order to accept and complete Step One, you need to acknowledge that these old ways simply don't work. They only delay the necessary first step of admitting what's true about the power your addictions have over you and the consequences as evidenced in your life.

- What are three ways you have tried to cope with or manage your addictions? How did these attempts leave room for you to continue with your addictions?

- What are three ways you have deceived yourself regarding the power your addictions have in your life? What excuses or false beliefs did you tell yourself in order to continue relying on your addictions?

- What are three ways you have deceived others regarding the extent and damage of your addictions? What excuses, lies, and stories did you often tell those closest to you in order to hide your addictions?

- What and who have you blamed for your life being unmanageable rather than confront the truth about the consequences of your addictions?

It's essential for you to acknowledge that you're powerless over your addictions and that your life is unmanageable for the very same reason that it's so painful to do so—namely, your ego. We all have one, and they all seem to operate in similar ways, helping us to keep our own self-interests front and center. Basically, your ego wants the world and everyone in it to do what you want, the way you want, and when you want it done.

You may not have identified it as your ego, but I bet you know that little inner voice in your head. It's the one that notices when others are not doing things that serve your best interests. When others don't recognize how special you are and don't drop everything to satisfy your every want and need, that voice tries to take the edge off your pain and disappointment by tilting you toward anger, resentment, payback, put-downs, and self-elevation.

Moreover, your ego wants you to believe you have far more power and control over your life than you actually do. Your ego tells you that you're the producer, director, and EGOT-winning star in the ongoing reality show of your daily life. Framed in spiritual terms, your ego wants you to believe that you're God.

But you don't need to read the book of Genesis again to know how that turned out for Adam and Eve with that whole forbidden fruit thing. The serpent told them that eating it would make them like God—that God had told them not to eat it because he didn't want them being as powerful and cool as he was. So, Adam and Eve ate the fruit and quickly discovered the hard way that they were indeed *not* God and never would be.

We've all been chasing such divine power in our own particular forbidden fruit ever since. Our egos keep trying to get us to believe that somehow we can be in control. Countless spiritual teachers have taught that every human being is addicted to at least one thing—the disease of "wanting to play God" . . . of wanting to control and exercise dominion over everybody and everything. This is the core addiction—the one underlying all other addictions. The addiction to control is often hard to spot because we've been at it our entire lives. It's always there.

Acknowledging that life is not working like you want it to work often requires seeing how you've tried to rely on your addictions to placate your ego. *You should have gotten what you know you deserve,* your ego says, *but since you didn't, you should enjoy some quality comfort, escape, and distraction found in* _____ .

In the Twelve Steps meetings I attend, we like to say, "Your ego is not your amigo." Don't talk yourself out of what you know is true.

- How would you define your ego based on your experience and awareness of it? What is the primary connection between your ego and your addictions?

* In the past year, what are some ways you have tried to inappropriately exercise power and control over your life? How has your ego fueled these attempts?

* What forbidden-fruit benefits have your addictions claimed to provide for you? How have your addictions provided a payoff or temporary benefit?

* What aspect of your life seems unmanageable right now? What in particular is causing you discomfort, distress, disappointment, or despair?

CONNECTING WITH OTHERS

It's one thing to acknowledge you're powerless over your addictions and your life is unmanageable to *yourself*. But admitting the truth to *other people* takes it to another level. Regardless of how vulnerable, embarrassed, or even ashamed you might feel in sharing the truth of Step One with others, it will open up the power of another truth: *You are not alone on this journey.*

Not only are you not the only one on this journey of spiritual growth and personal wholeness, but you can also help others and allow them to help you. Early on, the founders of AA realized the power of admitting one's struggles, weaknesses, failures, and lapses in front of others who completely understood and accepted them. This is why I encourage you to participate in a group that meets regularly or attend a weekly (if not more often) Twelve Steps meeting. There is no substitute for sharing where you are and getting compassionate, encouraging input from others. Even if there is no cross talk or follow-up questions, just having witnesses engaged with your journey is meaningful validation.

So, for this first Step, make sharing its truth with other people a part of your practice.

- What is the most challenging part of accepting and engaging with Step One? Do you agree that going all in with Step One is essential to your success with the other Steps? Why or why not?

- What example from chapter 3 in *The Fix*, "Without a Paddle," resonates or stands out the most for you? Why do you suppose it strikes you this way?

- What associations, past experiences, and traumas make it more challenging for you to acknowledge powerlessness in regard to your addictions? How is admitting the truth about your powerlessness over your addictions oddly empowering?

- What is one example of how your addictions are making your life unmanageable right now? How does this example leave you feeling most of the time—weak, ashamed, afraid, angry, or something else?

- What question related to Step One would you ask someone who has been working the Steps for many years? Why this question?

For the next session: Read or review chapters 1–3 in *The Fix*. Before the next session, make sure you have read chapter 4, "Helplessly Hoping." If you are participating in a group study, choose one thing that stands out from all that you've been reading and reflecting on related to Step One to share at your next meeting.

2

BELIEVE IN A GREATER POWER

STEP TWO: Came to believe that a Power greater than ourselves could restore us to sanity.

Despite being powerless in a messy life, change is not entirely up to you.

Depending on where you are in relation to your addictions, Step One may have hit you like a cold-water slap in the face or an Arctic tsunami. Fortunately, Step Two moves you beyond this place and offers hope in something other than your own efforts. True, you're powerless and your life is off-kilter, but you're not beyond help. Why? Because there's another way besides white-knuckling it until the bridge of willpower collapses into the floodwaters of chaos. Embracing Step Two offers more hope than the P-word, "powerless," suggests.

You can change, your life can change, and things can get better.

If Step One required you to admit your powerlessness, then Step Two reveals where the power to change will come from—a spiritual source greater than you. Depending on past experiences and your disposition toward faith and spirituality, this thought might stop you in your HOKAs. You might assume this "Power greater than ourselves" to be synonymous with the Judeo-Christian God. But let's hit pause on that. Assuming the Twelve Steps focus on the traditional Almighty is reductive at best and inaccurate, or imprecise, at worst.

If you're already a person of strong faith, then you might feel relief or anticipate having a head start on this whole recovery journey. Or you may have all kinds of good reasons for being skittish about how to relate to God and all you associate with spirituality as you've experienced it. You may have grown up in a religious tradition that has now failed you, leaving a gap between what you once believed and what you have now encountered in life. At this point, you might cherish your agnosticism or exult in your atheism.

Thankfully, the Twelve Steps offer a way forward not only for those who want a proven tool for strengthening their spiritual lives within their religious traditions but also for those who have given up on the idea of God and the church, who have moved beyond the religion of their childhood, or who have suffered spiritual trauma and are no longer sure if or what they believe anymore. Yep, basically everybody—including *you*.

This is why the exact wording of Step Two is important. Notice that it says, "came to believe" and not simply "believed." This is a crucial distinction that spotlights the *process* of growing spiritually rather than a simple one-and-done decision based on intellectual assent or emotional attachment. In other words, you don't have to have it figured out or even know exactly who or what you believe in. Maybe it's even better if you don't, at least in the beginning.

In fact, I trust the truth of Step Two because it *doesn't* promise overnight change or instantaneous relief simply because we're willing to consider belief in a Greater Power. Step Two simply indicates this spiritual process of trusting in a Greater Power will restore us to sanity. You've probably heard that the definition of insanity is doing the same thing repeatedly and expecting different results. Doing the Two Step, however, changes this dance because now you have a Greater Partner to lead you and restore you to wholeness.

- What rises up inside when you consider "a Power greater" than yourself? Which past experiences, events, and relationships influence your response as you consider coming to believe in a Greater Power that can restore you to sanity?

- How difficult is it for you to acknowledge that you need sanity restored in your life? What are some signs that your sense of peace, balance, and wholeness has been lacking?

- How have you experienced your spirituality as an ongoing process rather than a static conclusion or intellectual understanding? Where do you think you are now in your spiritual journey?

- What evidence do you see in your life that your addiction or compulsive behavior disrupts your sanity? What recurrent patterns or ongoing challenges emerge because of your relationship with your addictive coping strategy?

MEETING YOU WHERE YOU ARE

Step Two invites you to enter and engage in a spiritual relationship. After acknowledging your own efforts aren't working, you're offered an opportunity to surrender self-reliance and instead seek a Greater Power—in any way you perceive, imagine, describe, or want to pursue that Power. There's no rush or pressure to figure it out. You have the freedom and flexibility to suspend previous ideas of God and spirituality and open yourself to a new approach.

This freedom and flexibility was inherent in the Twelve Steps from the start. Bill Wilson noted that the "Realm of the Spirit is broad, roomy, all inclusive; never exclusive or forbidding to those who earnestly seek."[1] Your Greater Power doesn't require you to do anything other than engage in the process of being open to believe in more than yourself. In fact, the only nonnegotiable is that *this ultimate Power cannot be you*. While you may be a reasonably decent person, your track record proves you're a woefully deficient deity.

If you're presently a spiritual seeker, the only thing required of you in this Step is a *willingness* to believe there's something or someone bigger than you in the cosmos that can restore your particular brand of crazy. That's it! You don't have to believe anything specific about God right now. Just be *willing* to believe.

In addition to willingness, Bill Wilson indicated that Step Two also requires *openness:* a suspension of what you think you know and accept as absolute based on your past experience. This aspect of Step Two reminds me of what Japanese Buddhists call *shoshin,* which means "beginner's mind"—an open, curious orientation toward the world. Those who embrace a beginner's mind are free from preconceptions and prejudices. They are free and present to observe and explore things as they are rather than through the lens of their preexisting biases.

With this mindset, you become more playful, easily amazed and delighted, and open to new possibilities and fresh insights into life. You don't approach things with a fixed point of view but always ask, "To what new way of seeing the world do I need to avail myself?"

Jesus taught this same principle, though he might have called it "child's mind," as in "unless you return to square one and start over like children, you're not even going to get a look at the kingdom" (Matthew 18:3 MSG). Whether you identify as a Christian or not, you will find this mindset helpful as you embark on a new and distinctly different spiritual path than what has come before.

"Coming to believe" means giving a Greater Power consent to introduce you to spirituality in fresh ways. When you seek a new perspective on the divine, you realize there's still so much you don't know about everything. Strange and wonderful things will happen when you're open (again, not convinced, certain, or committed yet) to entertain the notion that a Greater Power exists and is eager to help you restore sanity in your life.

- On a scale of 1 to 10, with 1 being "so uncomfortable your skin crawls" and 10 being "completely and comfortably chill," what number reflects your willingness to believe in a Power greater than yourself? Briefly explain your choice.

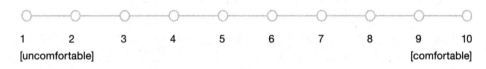

1   2   3   4   5   6   7   8   9   10

[uncomfortable]   [comfortable]

- What preconceived notions and personal assumptions do you have that could get in the way of you having an open and curious orientation toward the world—one that is free from preconceptions and prejudices? What do you need to suspend or release in order to get past these preconceived notions and assumptions?

- How would you describe what it means to have a "beginner's" or "child's" mind when it comes to the way you perceive the world? What would that look like?

MOVING FORWARD

Step Two says a Power greater than you can restore you to sanity.

While you may have a good idea of what crazy looks like, consider that the word *sanity* is derived from the Latin *sanus*, which literally means wholeness or health. So, if you're restored to a healthy place of being whole, you will no longer be fragmented or divided by the push-pull belief that your substance or compulsive behavior of choice can take away your unresolved traumas or feelings of spiritual homesickness. If you're not relying on the focus of your addictions to distract, numb, and pleasure you away from what's true and necessary for your sanity, it becomes easier to recognize how certain crazy assumptions have poisoned your thinking and hijacked your feelings.

This notion might seem like a big pill to swallow without a prescription. Perhaps you take issue with the implication that if a Greater Power can restore your sanity, you must be wrestling with the throes of *insanity* at present. But if you put mental health diagnostics and associations aside, you can see that insanity is simply brokenness—a lack of health and wholeness. No matter how well hidden you think it is, chaos inevitably results when you're snared by addiction.

If you draw on the premise of Step One again as you consider Step Two, you will likely be able to acknowledge the specific ways that powerlessness and unmanageability have manifested in your life. Just consider the number of times you've tried to give up your addiction only to yield to temptation and relapse. Think for a moment: When was the last time you said that this time would be the *last time* using your substance or behavior of choice? How often have you quit trying to give up your reliance on these other substances and behaviors because resisting your addictive impulse feels futile?

Addictions thrive because they provide momentary relief with diminishing returns. Your mind and body remember the relief from the pain when you ate that pint of gelato at bedtime, not to mention the pleasurable reinforcement of some exquisite chocolate. But eventually, a pint is not enough and you can hardly taste the flavor. So why not eat more and try other flavors? Even after you quit trying to deny the truth, you still return to the freezer . . . hoping for more than you know Ben and Jerry can ever deliver.

Doesn't that sound like insanity to you?

All human beings are addicted to their habitual and predictable patterns of crazy thinking. We attach and identify with our thoughts, and no matter how hard we try, we can't seem to change them . . . particularly those that hurt us. We assign meaning and value to those thoughts that they don't deserve. After a while, those thoughts become who we are rather than bubbles passing on the surface of the river of our consciousness. The only way to stop the continual chatter is to focus on the compassion, acceptance, understanding, and love of a Power greater than ourselves.

- How accurately does *insanity* describe or define your experience relating to your addiction? What other words or phrases come to mind?

- What thoughts and behaviors do you tend to repeat over and over again as part of your cycle of addiction? While experts have mapped the general sequence, write out or diagram your progression of thoughts and behaviors you usually follow when relying on your addiction.

- What thoughts, judgments, and assumptions recur in your mind because of your battle with addiction? Write down all the labels, critical statements, and shaming assessments that pop into your mind again and again.

- What are some ways you can see a Greater Power helping you with these intrusive thoughts and negative self-talk? What positive statements and affirmations would you like to replace the old tapes?

- What would your life look like if a Greater Power restored it to sanity? How do you imagine yourself and your life being when healthy and whole?

CONNECTING WITH OTHERS

You likely have no problem identifying the behaviors and thinking patterns in *others* that hold them back—even as you struggle to see how your own continue to disrupt your life. Which is a good reminder that you can't live out the Twelve Steps, including Step Two, alone. You need the support, encouragement, and perspective afforded by others who can relate to being addicted and also offer more objective perspective on your own battles. Working the Steps in community with others on a similar journey also helps you experience a Greater Power.

This is because one of the greatest benefits of connecting with others is *hope*. Most people, from neuroscientists to bartenders, acknowledge the necessity of hope to sustain the human spirit. While hope is one of the great intangibles in life, you know when you have it. There's a sense of moving out of the dark confinement of what your life has become and into an expansive place of freedom and discovery. Hope provides fuel for your willingness and openness toward God or your Greater Power: "Now faith is the assurance of things hoped for, the conviction of things not seen" (Hebrews 11:1 ESV).

From the horrors of concentration camps to the devastation of disease, hope keeps us willing to persevere and survive what presently feels unbearable. Hope does the same for addicts and those who are seeking something spiritually uplifting to elevate them from where they are to where they want to go. When others remind us that they've been where we are, we realize that we're not alone and find hope enough to persevere.

- What's the most challenging part of accepting and building on Step Two? What do you need in order to shift your spirituality in a new direction?

- Which example or story from chapter 4 in *The Fix*, "Helplessly Hoping," resonates with or jumps out for you? Why does that especially resonate with you?

- How would you describe your understanding of God at this age and stage of your life? How is your description and understanding colored by previous experiences, past associations, and religious traumas?

- When was the last time you felt like you were going crazy because of your addiction and compulsive behaviors? How frequently do you recognize the toll your struggles have on your relationships?

- What question would you ask your Greater Power if you could sit down face-to-face and talk right now? What do you imagine the response would be?

For the next session: Before moving forward, make sure that you have read through chapter 5, "Somebody Take the Wheel,s" in *The Fix*. If you are participating in a group study, choose one thing that stands out from all that you've been reading and reflecting on related to Step Two to share at your next meeting.

3

DECIDE TO TURN

STEP THREE: Made a decision to turn our will and our lives over to the care of God as we understood Him.

Step Three is known as the "surrender step," the "jumping-off point," the "wake-up call," or the "turning point," as Bill W. called it. Step Three is the foundation on which you build the rest of your Steps for recovery. If this Step sounds daunting, it's because it is—but it's also effortless. Many people who work the Twelve Steps cite this one as being the place they began "letting go and letting God."

Now, before you roll your eyes at such a coffee-mug cliché, I want to encourage you to visualize this adage in a way that is more concrete and tangible. Whether you imagine holding on to the edge of a cliff by your fingernails or squeezing the end of your rope until your hands bleed, try to see it . . . feel it . . . and then open your palms and let go! Only, you're not free-falling once you let go. Someone bigger and stronger, kinder and gentler, more powerful and more compassionate, immediately catches you. And you let yourself be caught—you don't flail or fight or try to resist. You take a deep breath and realize you're okay. God has got you. You can trust in him and rest in this knowledge.

Some folks describe the progression of these first three Steps like this: "I can't [Step One], but God can [Step Two], and I think I'll let him [Step Three]." If you think about it, that's the essence of the gospel message distilled into its simplest form. Or, if that's not helpful, just consider that Step Three spotlights the fact that you're not participating in a self-help program. You're way past the point of believing you can fix your addiction and how it's messed up your life. Your willpower, your good intentions, and even your sponsors and accountability partners—nothing and no one human being—can navigate the whitewater rapids churning within your ego's insistence on self-sabotage.

If you're not ready to jump into that transition truth of Step Three, then return to Step One and start over. Seriously, there's no shame if you're not ready to take the plunge. I remember one time seeing cliff divers training along the rocky coast of a beautiful beach. They would gradually go higher to the next tier, but not until they had confidently mastered the previous one. A couple times I saw a diver wait on the edge of one of the steeper cliffs before descending to a lower one. Mentally, he knew he wasn't ready yet.

So don't feel bad if this is what you have to do. Spiritual journeys often go backward before going forward again, or they take detours and go in circles. Your recovery is not a race, and there's no right way other than to engage the truth of each one. What's more, if you can't accept Step Three *wholeheartedly*, then the ones after it will seem like a dead end.

Step Three, like Steps One and Two, does not reflect defeat—it signals your willingness to try a new and different direction. If you're driving a familiar route and then one day the highway is blocked and there's nowhere to go except careening off-road through dirt tracks and overgrown lanes, you're going to get lost. You need a GPS, and assuming you can still get a signal, you'd be thrilled to follow its directions to where you want to go.

Step Three is a similar juncture. After the two previous Steps, you realize the only way to go forward requires letting Somebody else take the wheel. You don't have control of your life when in the throes of addiction, so why not try a spiritual connection to a Higher Power? You might be amazed at the freedom that comes from being tethered by faith to the power of supernatural love.

- What apprehensions do you have about embarking on Step Three? What do you imagine will happen if you let go and let God take control of your direction?

- What do you fear you will *lose* if you surrender your will and turn your life over to God or your Greater Power? What potential benefits and rewards are there?

- When have you taken a step of faith or risked trusting someone or something else in order to get what you needed? What did you learn—about yourself and about God—from that experience?

- What feelings and thoughts are triggered when you consider relinquishing control and surrendering your will? What past experiences and traumas influence your response to taking Step Three?

MEETING YOU WHERE YOU ARE

I'm guessing you've observed people who are committed, maybe even addicted, to spirit-building. Much like bodybuilders who work out constantly to attain the physical results they want, spirit-builders are always chasing the latest guru, enlightenment experience, spiritual retreat, inspirational book, church, temple, synagogue, or group. If they're Christians, then they're busting their tails to lead a godly life. No surprise, though, that they are continually exhausted and feel like enough is never enough. They may feel like a huge disappointment to the Divine, a poser, or, worse still, a hypocrite. They're well-intended but they're missing the on-ramp to spiritual awakening—it's not up to them!

When a person tells me they're trying to be "more spiritual" or "a better follower of Jesus," I tend to suspect they don't understand the gospel—that their devious little ego has hijacked their journey. Their efforts, either intentionally or subconsciously, rely on their own power in hopes of achieving something that can only be experienced through surrender. (The great irony of faith, right?)

Too often, we make faith so much harder than it is—because the only thing we really have to do is to stop doing everything. The essence of the gospel is so easy that we make it hard. It's not about reforming ourselves by what we do; it's about being transformed by a Greater Power to do for us what we simply cannot humanly do. There's no better synonym for the word *faith* than "let go!"

When we rely solely on our own efforts to give up our addictions and restore our sanity, we fail. Every time. When we try to change ourselves into the likeness of Jesus by following a checklist, we oppose the gospel of grace. Relying on our own efforts alone for spiritual awakening and growth becomes legalism, a merit-system marathon which we can never complete, let alone win.

Grace kicks in when we finally give up trying to fix ourselves—when we turn our will and our lives over to the care of God (as we understand him) and let divine love carry us. When we surrender and trust in a Higher Spiritual Power, we accept our human limitations and acknowledge that we need divine help. Imagine swimming and getting caught in the undertow of a riptide. You swim harder and faster but get nowhere, only ending up more exhausted and afraid. Then you finally stop and discover that you can float. Rather than fighting the current, you let it carry you back to shore. Perhaps it's time to try positioning yourself in that section of the river where the current of grace runs deepest and swiftest and then lie on your back and relax.

Step Three requires a leap of faith—but it's one that you can begin with baby steps. The great paradox of faith is that when you finally give up and acknowledge you can't keep going, you discover the power to persevere. You awaken to spiritual transformation.

- When have you found yourself focused on spirit-building by working harder and trying new methods? What caused you to realize that you can never do enough to attain the peace, joy, and faith you long to have?

- How can committing to Step Three—surrendering your will and life over to God's care—change the way you're living right now, today? What can you immediately stop doing and discard?

- What "terms of surrender" do you expect (or have already experienced) when you place your trust in God? What do you think your Greater Power requires of you once you're willing to trust him with your life?

- After you decide to surrender control of your life to God, how can you discern what you're supposed to do on a daily basis? How can you distinguish between being prompted by your Higher Power and the insistent voice of your ego?

MOVING FORWARD

Step Three could be your spiritual stepping stone to a healthier, happier, more peaceful, more satisfying life. Right now could be a watershed moment for you. If you're ready to let go and surrender your addiction and self-limiting compulsions to the care of God as you understand him, then you will experience a shift in how you live. If you're prepared to say, "Yep, I give up. I can't do it my way any longer. Here, God, please take my will and my life," then you can trust him to do it. Making this conscious choice to surrender means that you're about to experience a better life of sobriety, freedom, peace, and wholeness.

If I might make a suggestion, I encourage you to reflect on your expectations of what will happen *after* you surrender and let go of those as well. Even if you're a Christian and feel confident in your beliefs about God, Jesus, the Holy Spirit, sanctification, and transformation, and even if you feel like you surrendered a long time ago and have faith all figured out and know exactly where God wants you, I suggest putting those aside for now.

Instead, consider remaining open, humbly and earnestly, to all that remains unknown to you. If you sincerely believe God's ways are higher than your human ways—and if you're willing to acknowledge that your Greater Power has, well, greater power—then open your mind and heart to new possibilities. You see, your ego might be tempted to spot an escape hatch hiding in Step Three, one that allows you to derail the experiential benefit of working the Twelve Steps by assuming you know how God is and how he wants to move in your life. These ego-based, faulty assumptions may have been reinforced by other people, including other practitioners of the Twelve Steps.

Moving forward, going from Step Three to Step Four and beyond requires a child's heart and a beginner's mind. It requires a willingness to humbly let go of what you've assumed are certainties and allow for new perspectives on eternal truth. Step Three means you're choosing to trust what God has for you right now—not what you think he should have for you based on past experiences.

Maybe you feel as if you're dumbing down your intellect in order to take a chance on the unknown. Trust me, you're not—you're just being wise enough to realize that intellect isn't enough. Nothing you possess can empower you the way your Higher Power can empower you. Recognizing your human limitations and personal weaknesses will clear your path to walk into a new season of faith-based sobriety.

And here's the thing: no matter where you are, if you're willing to let go, then you can trust that real, sustainable change has begun. You may understand precious little about God, or you may think you know a lot, but either way, if you're willing to get on your knees and ask him to remove your reliance on alcohol, drugs, work, codependent behaviors, harmful relationships, sex, porn, overeating, people-pleasing, sports betting, or whatever your thing is, then you must know one thing is certain: *he will do it.*

- List three specific changes you *hope* (not *think* or *expect*) that God will make in your life once you've surrendered your will and control to him.

    1. _____

    2. _____

    3. _____

- Which of those three changes can only occur through some power greater than your own? In other words, how can you know that God is at work in your life?

- We've used several metaphors for surrendering your will and turning your life over to God's care—including cliff-diving, swimming in a riptide, and off-road navigation. Besides these, what would you compare to this process of acting on Step Three? What metaphor seems apt for where you are in your life right now?

- People working the Twelve Steps sometimes speak of Step Three as a "one-way door" or a passage that, once you've gone through it, doesn't allow you to return the same way. Think about this as you answer the next two questions.

> Assuming this comparison *doesn't* mean you won't struggle, relapse, or use again, what does it imply?

> How will your recovery process change as you consider Step Three and awaken to God's presence in your life?

CONNECTING WITH OTHERS

Once you move through Step Three, prepare to experience life and the world around you in richer, more vivid ways. Once I took this step, I found that everywhere I turned, I glimpsed God. Whether in the intricate beauty of the dogwood blossoms outside my window, the unexpected but spot-on words of encouragement from someone else in recovery, or the shift in my attitude when faced with disappointment, I knew God was working in me and in my life. My doubts evaporated as I became acutely aware that the world brims with grace. No longer did everything revolve around me, and not only was that okay, but it was also gloriously liberating.

Your relationships will also change after taking Step Three. You'll realize that you are no longer alone and have other kindred sojourners with whom to travel. Rather than isolate, brood, ruminate, or flirt with your old flame of addiction, you will find that you can push through pride and discomfort and ask for support. Some relationships may fall apart, mostly because they relied on unhealthy or destructive dynamics, but many more connections will strengthen and solidify. You will see God moving and working in the lives of others—including what you're able to give and offer them.

- How have your relationships already changed since you began this study and started working through these first three Steps? What's surprised you most about your interactions with others?

- Who is someone in recovery with a faith you admire? What in particular appeals to you about their spirituality?

- How do you experience God at your Twelve Steps meetings or other support group gatherings? How is God revealing himself to you through other people?

- What do you need most from other people as you take Step Three and move forward? Who, specifically, can you ask for what you need this week?

For the next session: Before moving on to Step Four, make sure that you have read or reviewed "Hug the Cactus," chapter 6 in *The Fix*. If you're part of a group study, choose at least one thing that resonates with you about Step Three to share at your next meeting.

4

TAKE INVENTORY

STEP FOUR: Made a searching and fearless moral inventory of ourselves.

With Step Four, everything changes.

You've reflected through Steps One and Two and made a conscious decision in Step Three to surrender your will and your life into God's care. Walking into Step Four, however, begins the more rigorous challenge of courageously digging below the surface—like, way below the surface and into the depths of all you've been carrying for most of your life. Your life is under new management, so it's important to acknowledge, assess, and eliminate all the accumulated junk you've buried. It's time to face the underlying causes and conditions fueling your addictions, all the resentments, fears, wounds, traumas—and the guilt, regret, and shame tagging alongside them.

This kind of excavation requires you to perform an autopsy on your past in order to experience new life through your Higher Power. No one particularly enjoys confronting their own self-centeredness—the petty grudges, bitter resentments, shameful secrets, and justified indulgences they usually keep locked up deep inside. But surrendering your will and life to God includes everything, including all the nasty stuff you'd rather ignore and take to your grave rather than acknowledge and reveal.

The purpose of Step Four is not for you to wallow, grovel, or shame yourself even more. You're stepping into the dense depths to face the truth in order to make room for who you really are and for all the good stuff God wants to pour into your life. As you begin awakening to the spiritual dimension of your recovery, you discover that making "a searching and fearless moral inventory" is not self-flagellation. Taking stock of your life compels you to take responsibility for what's yours, ask for God's help to move forward, and toss the rest.

Christians and other spiritual seekers often call this process *repentance*. I realize this word, along with its verb form *repent*, may present a minefield of memories involving altar calls, church camp, and street preachers. But repenting isn't about hating yourself because of how weak and wicked you are. It's about discovering and experiencing love—from God and for yourself.

Repentance is simply considering what will truly make you happy and recognizing all the ways that you've settled for so much less. It's a process of ongoing reflection about the false beliefs you've held and the lies you've accepted concerning who you really are and what you really need and want. It's looking at the story you are telling yourself and poking holes in it until you discover the true story that God is co-authoring with you. Like the prodigal son in Jesus' parable (told in Luke 15:11–32), you spiritually awaken and "come to your senses." Repentance is removing the blindfold you have been wearing for so long and now seeing what's true through the eyes of your heart.

Step Four, with its many lists and mandatory introspection, may feel like learning choreography for a Broadway show when all you want to do is sway to the music. But your sobriety and healing requires relentless honesty with yourself. You can't just skim the surface and move on. Yes, the process will break your heart at times in ways that seem unbearable. But as it does, you discover forgiveness, grace, mercy, empathy, and compassion shine through the cracks.

- Notice the three adjectives used in Step Four that describe your self-inventory: *searching*, *fearless*, and *moral*. What does each of these mean to you as you take a long, close look at how you got here? Which one of these three words causes you the most concern? Why?

- How much work have you done in terms of looking at traumatic milestones and turning points in your life? What aspects of your story have you already examined—and which ones require more attention?

- Generally, how would you describe your relationship with honesty? Are you prone to withhold or try to delete the hard parts of your life, or are you more likely to curate and exaggerate them in order to get others' attention and/or sympathy?

- What intimidates or worries you the most about completing Step Four? What are some ways that you can show yourself patience, kindness, and compassion in the midst of being unflinchingly honest with yourself?

MEETING YOU WHERE YOU ARE

Step Four is not one you can sleepwalk through—not that any of the others are. Working through this Step requires persistence, determination, and perseverance—a commitment to keep *searching* even when all the usual suspects have been identified. Step Four undoubtedly requires courage as well—being *fearless* in looking at what you'd rather not see. Note that being fearless does not mean you're not afraid, only that you're unwilling to let your fear stop you from digging and doing a thorough, comprehensive inventory.

This Step specifies taking a moral inventory as well—not just a list of events, conversations, situations, and traumas. At first glance, *moral* might seem harsh because it involves assessing right from wrong, good from bad, and nice from not-so-nice. But it transcends black-and-white categories and invites you to consider whether your past behavior aligns with your values. Have you been practicing what you say you believe, or have your struggles with addiction wedged an ever-widening gap between the two? Thinking through your core values before you begin making the various lists for your inventory might be helpful.

Part of the beauty of Step Four is that you can make it your own while knowing there's always more to do or review. There is no single, universally agreed-upon format or method for conducting your searching, fearless moral inventory. There may be as many ways as there are practitioners of the Twelve Steps. A great place to start, though—as well as a foundation you can revisit and build upon— is to focus on five key inventory lists: (1) Resentment Inventory, (2) Fear Inventory, (3) Sexual Conduct Inventory, (4) General Harms Done Inventory, and (5) "Skeletons in the Closet" or "Deathbed Secrets" Inventory. (Each of these inventories can be found in appendices A–E of this workbook.)

While there are variations, sub-inventories, and creative ways of extending your inventory, these five planks will form a strong platform for walking your Steps. And you will be returning and reviewing (and possibly revising and amending) these lists in Step Five through Step Nine. So the more thoughtful and thorough you are with them now, the better.

Many people in recovery doing the Steps, myself included, believe identifying and expressing your resentments offers fertile ground for beginning your excavation. As Bill Wilson explains, "Resentment is the 'number one' offender. It destroys more alcoholics [addicts] than anything else."[2] Perhaps you've never considered your resentment to be the dangerous criminal at the top of your emotional Most Wanted list. But if you think about it, someone stuck in the quicksand of resentment will have a tough time remaining sober.

This is because resentment thrives when you emotionally continue reliving a past injury as if it's reoccurring in the present. Resentment takes root when you experience injustice and plant seeds of bitterness, anger, and self-pity. When you're treated unfairly, you want others to notice and do something about it. You want an apology or compensation—or payback.

To shove a salt block into the wound, your Resentment Inventory requires a comprehensive list but doesn't stop there. You're also asked to reflect and write down what role *you* played in the episode that led to your resentment. In almost every case, according to *The Big Book* by Bill W., you played a part. What were your mistakes, faults, or character defects that played even a minor role in the creation of your resentment? Where were you self-seeking? When were you being dishonest? How were you acting out of fear, jealousy, or spite? Where were you at fault and accountable?

Coming clean about your deepest resentments isn't easy or pleasant. And your addictions and compulsive behaviors have done a good job of distancing you from your anger. But you will never find healing and freedom until you consciously confront your darkness. If you don't identify and integrate your shadow side, it will always threaten to eclipse the rest of you.

Take a moment now to complete the Resentment Inventory found at the back of this workbook. Give yourself ample time but try not to get stuck on any one part or incident for too long. And don't hold back! After you've completed it, answer the following questions.

- Looking at your list of resentments, you might notice some specific incidents that have led you to resent certain people, institutions, places, situations, and events. For example, you didn't get what you wanted for several birthdays while you were growing up so now you resent those times (and your family) for disappointing you, but you also resent yourself for having any expectations on your birthday now as an adult. List three of these connections between specific resentments from your past that continue to sustain presents resentments as well:

    1. _____

    2. _____

    3. _____

- Choose one of your most deep-seated resentments from your completed Inventory and then complete the following:

  I resent _____
  because _____
  and this affects _____
  which in turn activates _____ .

- As you recalled the catalysts for various resentments, which ones triggered the greatest emotional responses in the moment? What messages do these particular feelings convey about these resentments?

- How have your resentments contributed to your addictions and compulsive behaviors? Describe the patterns or connections you see between them.

MOVING FORWARD

While Bill W. believed that resentment and anger threaten a person's recovery the most, fear can't be far behind. Just as you didn't realize how many grudges and resentments you carry, you might have been surprised at the extent to which your fears, both conscious and unconscious, have kept you in an emotional vise.

Fear in itself is no fun, but it also trips the wires on all your character flaws and weaknesses. Follow a specific fear and see how you tend to compensate, hide, deceive, posture, manipulate, lie, or run from it. Fear pulls the strings on so many of the behaviors you're loathe to admit.

Perhaps you shift into one-up mode when you're around others you view as successful because you're afraid they won't accept you as their equal. Or maybe you tilt into OCD-type perfectionism when you have guests visit your home because you're afraid of how they might judge you based on where you live. Or perhaps you resort to anger as your go-to reaction whenever people ask you to add one more thing to your list because you're afraid of failing and disappointing them. It's easier to blow up at them for asking them to deal with your fear of not being able to do what they ask.

Fear often thrives when we're trying to manage life on our own. *The Big Book* describes fear as the result when "self-reliance failed us."[3] Depending on your level of self-awareness, your Fear Inventory might feel uncomfortable, to say the least. But that's also how you loosen the grip your fears have had on you.

As you relinquish control and trust your Greater Power, your fears will diminish or fade away completely. Faith is the antidote for the poison that fear feeds into your system. Relying on God rather than yourself leaves little room for fear to grow. In fact, the further you go into your Step Four inventory, the more you will realize that relying on God is the only way to get out from beneath all the burdens weighing you down.

So, take a moment now to complete the Fear Inventory found in the back of this workbook. Once again, take all the time you need without chasing too many fears that will derail your assessment. Step Four instructs you to make a fearless inventory, or, as I like to think of it, a "fear-less" inventory, because once you've completed it, you have less to fear. Once you've finished your Fear Inventory, use the following questions to study your results.

- Similar to the connections you made between past catalysts for resentment and their present manifestations, consider the links between your fears and unhealthy behaviors. List three of these fear-behavior correlations below:

  1. _____
  2. _____
  3. _____

- Now choose one of your biggest and most persistent fears from your completed Inventory. Then complete the following:

I welcome my fear of _____
because it signals _____ ,
which reminds me to rely on God for _____
_____
rather than what I used to do, which was _____
_____ .

- Which pervasive fears can you trace back to childhood events, conversations, traumas, and relationships? How can seeing the origin of these fears help you face them now?

- Which of your fears have been compounded by shame, regret, and insecurity? (For example, perhaps you're even more afraid of imposter syndrome because of the shame you feel from past times others have called you out.)

After cataloging your resentments and facing your fears, there's still plenty of work to do. So browse through the other inventory forms found in the back of this workbook and choose at least two more to complete before moving into Step Five. (For instance, doing a Sex Conduct Inventory might take shame to another level, but you will experience so much freedom and insight when it's done.)

From there, choose another inventory related to one of your greatest struggles, whether it's finances, violence and trauma, authority and power, or "skeletons in your closet." Each inventory will yield incredible insight into why you've been doing what you've been doing each time you spiral into your addictive cycles. And remember, you can do more and different inventories the next time you work your way through the Twelve Steps. In recovery, you become a lifelong student of yourself and what makes you tick.

CONNECTING WITH OTHERS

While doing the hard shoveling required for Step Four, you might sometimes feel like you're digging your own grave before falling into it. In fact, it's just the opposite. You're preventing yourself from being buried alive by the weight of all these layers pressing you down. But getting out of this pit requires help, which leads right into Step Five.

Before going into the Step Five confessional, though, don't hesitate to ask for support, prayer, encouragement, and wisdom from others who have already worked Step Four and returned Lazarus-like from the grave of their resentments, fears, weaknesses, and failures. They know firsthand how excruciating it can be to dig up the ugly corpses of the past and look at them in the light. But they also know the pain is more than worth it.

Particularly, if you feel stuck while completing one of the inventory forms, reach out to someone you trust—preferably someone also in recovery who's ahead of you in the Steps—and let him or her know where you are. Risk being vulnerable about what you're feeling and the temptation to shut down (also known as dissociating) and/or act out (also known as relapsing). Know that the other person is hearing you, seeing you, and offering you a hand up. Don't be afraid to take it or resent yourself for needing help.

One final point for you to consider: As you complete parts of your inventory, you may be tempted to edit, withhold, revise, or curate your responses—especially if you're aware you will be sharing your answers with someone in Step Five. So revisit your lists and see if you find evidence of where you've filtered your work because of what others might think. Make any necessary corrections so that you're left with the unvarnished truth.

* Review the inventory you've been doing for Step Four and notice the relationships that appear on your lists. You will probably notice a few recurring characters as well as cameos from people you didn't realize you resented, feared, hated, loved, or used. List them below and note the inventory lists on which they pop up.

Person	Inventory list

- Who would you want to make sure *never* sees your Step Four inventory? Why do you fear their response? Check all that apply and feel free to add your own.

  ☐ They couldn't possibly understand.
  ☐ They would think so much less of me.
  ☐ Their judgment would feel unbearable to me.
  ☐ Their disappointment would crush me.
  ☐ Their rejection and abandonment—enough said!
  ☐ They would no longer trust me.
  ☐ They would realize I've betrayed them.
  ☐ They would hate me for hurting them and others.
  ☐ They would only add to my shame.
  ☐ They don't know about my addictions.
  ☐ Their pity and condescension aren't helpful.
  ☐ Other concerns:

- You might be tempted to procrastinate, postpone, or quit working through Step Four before completing all facets of your comprehensive inventory. How can you help yourself follow through and keep going? What do you need from your Higher Power in order to continue working through the Steps?

For the next session: Get ready to "Fess Up" by reading or reviewing chapter 7 of the same name in *The Fix*. If you're participating in a group study, choose one item from any of your Step Four inventory work to share at your next meeting.

5

ADMIT THE WRONGS

STEP FIVE: Admitted to God, to ourselves, and to another human being the exact nature of our wrongs.

Congratulations—if you're reading this, then you completed Step Four!

While I celebrate your hard work, now it's time to take it to another level. As hard as it was to get through Step Four, Step Five is even harder. Don't let this discourage you, though, because for my money, this Step might be the most exhilarating to complete. When you've gone deep and assessed the hardest chapters in your story, you experience relief and satisfaction. When you share the narrative that's emerged, you are no longer alone. You have a divine witness as well as a human one, not to mention more compassion, I hope, for yourself.

After making "a searching and fearless moral inventory" of yourself in Step Four, you're now instructed to go full frontal and admit "the exact nature of your wrongs" not only to God (which isn't so bad because he already knows, right?) and to yourself (no spoiler alert necessary) but to another human being (usually not a random stranger). While you may be tempted to check off the first two and leave the third admission indefinitely hanging, don't postpone one of the greatest gifts of the Twelve Steps: telling your story, being known, and being accepted.

You rob yourself if you skip completing the Step Five hat trick—sharing your story with God, yourself, and another human. As long as you refuse to bring your secrets into the light, you will remain ashamed, conflicted, and afraid you can never be known and loved. When you isolate yourself and remain the only one who knows the real story, you get in the way of your own recovery. Freedom from the root causes and underlying conditions feeding your addictions and compulsive behaviors requires telling the truth—all of it, not just 87 percent.

Everyone has a story. And while your story might defy genre classification on Netflix, it's all yours—and it's far from over. No matter how painful, raw, humiliating, and wrenching some of the moments might seem, your story is sacred. It has brought you to where you are right now. You deserve to have your story heard, not only for your own benefit but also for your listeners.

As a student of C. S. Lewis said to him in the movie *Shadowlands*, "We read to know we're not alone."[4] We share our stories with one another for the same reason. When you tell your story, others recognize themselves in your experience and feel the freedom to in turn share their own. Which is what Step Five is really all about—sacred storytelling.

Sure, your ego will try to edit, revise, exaggerate, and embellish your story so that you look better than the monster you think you are. Truth is, you're a mixed bag. As human beings, we contain more contradictions within ourselves than we know what to do with most of the time. We're selfish and still want to love others. We're petty and also generous. We're liars desperate to tell the truth about our lying. Our egos prefer to Photoshop our public persona and keep all the warts and blemishes in a trash file. Admitting what's true, however, encompasses all that's true, including—especially—the contradictions. Yes, you're weird, but so am I. And guess what? We all are!

Step Five helps you reenter the human race and connect with everyone else who thinks they're the worst. In order to get better, we dispel our shame and walk alongside those around us. We don't have to be better-than or worse-than, one-up or one-down. Step Five levels the playing field and defeats all the guilt, shame, and loneliness inside—leaving us lighter as we step into freedom.

- How is your ego trying to thwart your progress? What are some tactics your ego previously used for hiding your addictions and skirting the painful truth?

- After you've admitted "the exact nature of your wrongs" to God or your Higher Power, what do you imagine will be the response? What do you want to hear or receive from the Divine?

- How have you related to yourself in light of completing the comprehensive inventory in Step Four? Have you tended to tilt more toward being critical or compassionate, more ashamed or more accepting, more entitled or more enlightened toward yourself? Explain your response.

- When you consider sharing your story with another person, what rises up inside? What feelings, expectations, and concerns do you need to address internally before confessing to someone else?

MEETING YOU WHERE YOU ARE

If Step Four unlocks the prison of your past, then Step Five opens the door and beckons you forward into your future freedom. You've looked into the abyss of your own darkness, and now it's time to illuminate the path forward by gazing beyond yourself. In full possession of the whole truth and nothing but the truth, Step Five allows you to ease the weight of this burden by off-loading it, exorcising it by admission with God and then yourself and then with another person. This progression is intentionally progressive and helps build trust in others as well as contextual perspective.

The first two admissions may seem redundant at first glance. Steps Two and Three awakened a new spiritual perspective and awareness of God's presence permeating your life. Steps One and Four acknowledged the humbling truth of your situation. So why do you need to admit your faults, flaws, and failures to God and then to yourself? The reason is because this forces you to take ownership and then release it, to admit the truth and then to let it breathe in your relationship with your Greater Power and within yourself.

You may be tempted to go through the motions of confessing what's up with your addictions with God without actually engaging with him. After all, he's inherently omniscient, and even if you doubt that, you've already surrendered your will and your life to him, which includes an all-access pass to the items in your inventory. Unless you're willing to speak from your heart and include the gory details, you're likely avoiding the gravity of your story. And when you distance yourself from your shadow, you undermine the power of grace and the value of forgiveness. Admitting the exact nature of your wrongs—not the general gist or greatest hits or CliffsNotes—reminds you of why you surrendered to God and why you will need to continue relying on him.

Sharing the exact nature of your wrongs with yourself forces you to take a step back and look at the big picture so you realize where you are in relation to the all that's gone before. When you can take in the totality of all your inventory revealed, you start seeing connections between what has happened to you and your reactions, responses, and choices. With your ego-alarm disabled, you begin noticing your hidden motives, false assumptions, and mistaken beliefs—all the old thoughts that frequently pinball around your mind.

Similar to completing and assessing your inventory in Step Four, your self-admission in Step Five is not about kicking yourself while you're down, forging weapons of self-destruction, or shaming yourself for not feeling more shame. Step Five is about accessing freedom. Knowing the truth is not enough—to be set free requires allowing others to know it too.

- What past experiences and associations do you have with the concept of "confession"? What is different and distinct about the kind of confession that Step Five is asking you to do?

- What are some ways you can avoid going through the motions when admitting the exact nature of your wrongs to God? What time, place, and setting would help you engage your full attention as you confess to your Higher Power?

- If you were pitching your life story as a movie or limited series, what would you title it? Why that title? How would you describe it in a couple of sentences?

- How would you want this movie or series to end? Where do you imagine your story going now that you've surrendered to God and asked him to co-author it?

MOVING FORWARD

One of the greatest benefits of the Twelve Steps emerges from taking the fifth Step. The sense of relief, connection, forgiveness, and acceptance you experience when sharing your story with another living, breathing human being is beyond compare. When you release your darkest, dirtiest secrets and confess your strangest, saddest moments of moral failure to someone else who listens and receives everything you say with compassion, you are set free.

So often we carry around this notion that if anyone discovered the truth about us they would recoil at seeing the inhuman animal we are, run screaming from the room, and call the Vatican for immediate exorcism and intervention. Your ego is probably playing movie trailers for this horror flick on the screen of your mind about now. *Why would I dare tell anyone all the wrongful things I've done? What could I possibly gain from exposing myself with such raw, naked, unflattering vulnerability? Don't you think it would sabotage my recovery if I let someone else see me this way?* These are the insidious questions your ego uses to wedge you into wavering as you cross the Step Five bridge.

But you're stronger and more courageous than your ego realizes, because you're no longer relying on your own willpower, determination, and shame-based logic. You've already surrendered all that and more to your Higher Power. You're trusting in that Power to continue meeting you where you are and leading you forward into a promised land you can never reach by yourself. In fact, don't take my word for it, take God's. Scripture makes the benefit of admitting your faults to someone else plain and simple: "Confess your sins to each other and pray for each other so that you may be healed" (James 5:16). Bill Wilson was inspired in large part by this passage when he wrote Step Five. He knew confession is not only good for our souls but also essential on the road to recovery.

Both Bill W. and the apostle James realized that when we don't confess our sins to one another, we come down with a bad case of isolation, self-recrimination, and toxic shame. Admitting the exact nature of our wrongs facilitates healing and remedies our soul sickness with the power of the truth: we're not alone anymore, no one is judging us, and we're loved and forgiven. Step Five has been said to promote good spiritual hygiene because it removes all the mental, emotional, and spiritual gunk that accumulates and poisons us. But this cleansing requires admitting the truth in order for us to get it out of our system and receive grace, mercy, forgiveness, and hope in its place.

Ultimately, completing Step Five helps you become fully human again. Just like Pinocchio became a real boy once he admitted his folly and received the love of Geppetto, you realize that you're not the worst offender in the human race and that you struggle pretty much like everyone else. Best of all, you don't have to remain mired in place by the weight of it all any longer.

While the person listening to your Step Five–prompted confession doesn't have the spiritual authority to forgive you completely or grant you absolution, that person can give you what's often called "an assurance of pardon." In other words, you can know that you're forgivable. Completing this fifth Step relieves you of the burdens you've been carrying and ushers you into the fullness of your spiritual awakening.

- If you allow your imagination to run wild, what's the worst thing that could possibly happen when you share your story with someone else? Looking at this possibility with more objectivity, where do you see your fears creeping in?

- Now take a deep breath and imagine the best-case scenario—one in which you tell the complete truth without the other person flinching. What do you hope to gain from this experience? What would you like to receive from this person in his or her expression, body language, and verbal response to what you share?

- Who will you become if you're not carrying around the ball and chain of your past transgressions? What will your life look like once you complete Step Five?

- How will you deal with moving into the uncharted territory of grace and freedom after working Step Five? How will this process enable you to be your authentic self (and not your ego) more fully?

CONNECTING WITH OTHERS

It's tough to know who to choose to hear your admission when completing Step Five, particularly if it's your first time doing it. While the listener you choose doesn't need professional credentials or spiritual authority, this individual does need to be willing, trustworthy, and nonjudgmental. Which is why, in my experience, broken people who have been set free often make the best confessors.

When people have endured suffering and brokenness in their own lives, they have humility and compassion for others traveling a similar rocky road. Nothing you say will shock them because they're well aware of their own messiness and aren't trying to hide behind self-righteousness, perfectionism, or moral superiority. They get you because they've stepped where you're now stepping.

Obviously, if you have a sponsor, he or she is a prime candidate. But as you work through Step Five, you can also share your story with your counselor, therapist, pastor, spiritual director, or a longtime friend whom you completely trust. If this person is unfamiliar with the Steps, you will find instructions to share with them in appendix F at the back of this workbook. This summarizes the purpose of Step Five, their unique role, and how best to help you.

- Who are the top three contenders you're considering to receive your confession? List their names below and give a brief summary of why you trust them.

Person	Why you trust him or her

- What qualities and character traits do you want your confessor to possess to help you feel heard, known, accepted, and assured of pardon? How important is it to you that they are in recovery and have completed their own Step Five?

- Thinking about logistics and details, what do you need for this to happen? How can you create a safe, relaxed environment with the privacy and lack of distractions and interruptions necessary for confessing to this other person?

- Imagine that you're hearing the confession of another person in recovery. What would you want to tell that person after he or she has finished sharing? What benediction or blessing would you offer to that person?

For the next session: Read or review chapter 8, "Okay, I'm Willing Already," in *The Fix*. If you're participating in a group study, consider sharing three words that best describe your experience admitting to another human being the exact nature of your wrongs. This, of course, assumes you will complete Step Five (admitting to God, yourself, and another human being) before moving on.

6

RELEASE THE DEFECTS

**STEP SIX: Were entirely ready to have God remove
all these defects of character.**

You might feel exhausted after the intense hard work you've done to complete Steps Four and Five. You probably feel like you need a break . . . a respite to catch your spiritual and emotional breath before getting the second wind you need to continue. Step Six offers you this opportunity for rest but at a price—your old ways of coping under stress, also known as your addictions, are relinquished once more as you double down on spiritual renewal.

Step Six (and its non-identical twin, Step Seven, which we will explore next) requires a sincere desire to change at a molecular level. This change isn't about becoming someone else but about embracing the essence of who God created you to be. After all, why would you hesitate to let God remove all your "defects of character"? Who doesn't want to show up as their best self, right?

Keep in mind, though, that we're not talking about fairy-tale magic where all your frogs are taken away and transformed into princes. Completing this Step doesn't involve reciting a Harry Potter spell or rubbing a magic lamp. It's not even about attending another meeting or praying the Serenity Prayer. The key to effectively working Step Six is twofold: (1) going all in and being "entirely ready" to change; and (2) letting honesty and truth become your filters for identifying your "defects of character."

If you haven't realized it by now, there's nothing haphazard or random about the specific language expressing each Step. So including the adverb "entirely" before "ready" is not redundant, bad form, or poor construction. It underscores the fact that you might think you're ready, and might actually be prepared to move forward, but that it's time to remove the ego net as you traverse the high wire of faith-balanced recovery.

After completing the previous five Steps, you are now clear-eyed and sober to the reality of your story. You've admitted your powerless over your addictions and related compulsive behaviors and have come to believe that God or your Higher Power is your only hope. You've surrendered your will and entrusted your life to the care of this spiritual Power to the best of your understanding. In Step Four, you dug deep into the hard soil of your past and sifted through your resentments, fears, sexual history, anger, self-pity, and all the forms of selfishness you found there. Like an archaeologist finding the entrance to your personal pyramid, you stepped into the interior heart of your deficits, deficiencies, deprivations, and defects. You then shared your scary discoveries with God, yourself, and another person by completing Step Five.

Moving into Step Six is not a passive posture that assumes God will just reset your DNA. It's an active willingness, a comprehensive readiness, to move forward into a life not built on the wobbly debris of your past that's been supporting your addictions. Step Six requires you to yell out, "Yep, I'm ready for the wrecking ball! Have at it, God!" and get out of the way. No longer clinging to your addictions in reaction to your spiritual discomfort and the pain of unresolved past traumas, you're entrusting your character's remodel and renovation to the only contractor, your Higher Power, capable of completing such a feat.

- What does "entirely ready" mean to you? What's left for you to surrender and to embrace in order to be completely willing to change?

- When you think about your top-ten finalists for greatest character defects, which ones are near the top of your list? Which ones have caused the most collateral damage in your life and relationships? Be as specific as possible.

- Which of your character defects seems front and center right now as you consider asking God to remove it along with all your other defects? How might your ego be trying to use this defect to delay going all in with Step Six?

- Knowing all you know about yourself and the new direction you're taking recovery, how willing are you to live life without the familiarity of your character defects? What's preventing you from being 100 percent willing?

MEETING YOU WHERE YOU ARE

There's a brilliant inner logic to the Twelve Steps. They present the paradox of being like those stacking Russian dolls that require you to pry open one after another to get to what's inside while also building on each other in ways that leave you progressively stronger in your faith. Working the Steps allows you to see the errant thinking, disruptive emotions, and unmanageable behaviors fueling your addictions and to replace them with a lifelong process of living in clarity, sobriety, and spiritual fulfillment.

Step Six offers a clarion call to get serious, just in case you weren't already, about letting God do what has to be done in order for you to grow and heal from the moral deformity and addictive chaos of your character defects. You've sorted the accumulated clutter, cleared the spaces, and packed the moving truck—now it's time to wave goodbye as it drives away. You've awakened spiritually and made room in your life for God to work and transform you into more of who you really are. This, of course, is an ongoing process—along with all the Steps—rather than a one-and-done kind of move. Walking the Twelve Steps on your path of recovery requires taking Step Six on a daily basis.

Even though you consistently practice this sixth Step, you're also experiencing the impact of undergoing a major paradigm shift. Particularly, the first couple times you work through Step Six, you will notice a change in the way you think, the way you see, the way you talk and act, and the way you relate to others. It's not perfection—nothing is in this life—but it is real-time, real-life spiritual transformation already in progress. You're being changed from the inside out at a level you've likely never encountered before.

Why does allowing God to remove your character defects cause such radical change? One primary reason is because you now have spiritual room to grow. Your character defects ignited addictive behaviors that blocked the flow of God's love in you and through you into others. You're stuck in place and fixated on your addictions rather than your higher purpose. Your relationships can only go so far because you're operating out of fear, insecurity, comparison, competition, and manipulation. Once these defects have been spiritually bulldozed, you have a new site for reconstructing the truest version of you.

Keep in mind these defects aren't simply flaws in how you're wired. They almost always form as a result of wounding from life's traumas—from what you experienced that you should never have experienced and by what you didn't get that you needed for healthy emotional and personal development. For this reason, I prefer to think of these survival strategies as "character defenses" rather than defects. These defenses helped you survive throughout your childhood based on the data you had available at the time.

Your character defenses merely tried to provide what you needed to help you meet unmet needs—a way to survive the pain and chaos around you in an often unpredictable world. These self-survival tactics emerged and lodged inside you long before you had agency to see other options and make better choices. But now they're past their sell-by date and have the rancid smell of addiction. Letting your Higher Power take them gives you space for knowing better, healthier strategies based on being loved, forgiven, and empowered by faith.

* What do you believe you lose by giving up your character defects? And what will you gain by handing them over to your Higher Power?

* What are some healthy, positive ways to deal with the disorientation that may come as you relinquish these character defects? What can you focus on instead?

* What are some tangible ways and feasible practices for this ongoing process of spiritual transformation? What spiritual activities will help you grow in your faith?

* As you consider your defects as "character defenses," how did they help you survive earlier in your life? Why are they no longer viable as survival strategies— but instead are keeping you stuck in place with your addictions?

MOVING FORWARD

Working through Step Six is trickier than it first appears and includes a number of challenges you'll do well to anticipate. With a heads-up to be on the lookout for these sharp edges, you can make sure you avoid any cuts.

It's no shocker that your ego remains the primary terrorist threat to your spiritual growth and recovery. Even now that you're halfway through the Twelve Steps, your ego can't always be trusted to surrender peacefully. More likely, your ego just comes up with more sneaky and subtle ways to manipulate you into conforming to its demands. Without missing a beat, you might find yourself misreading Step Six as being "entirely ready to have your brilliant, talented self remove your character defects in its own power." Yeah, it's not going to work, but the ego still thinks you're willing to follow its lead.

Your ego also adapts quickly and can MacGyver makeshift tools for exploding your work in the Steps. With Step Six, you should look for ego-ignited blasts of *spiritual pride*. You know, like basking in how pleased your Higher Power must be to see you doing such a good job and being one of the best Step practitioners in the history of recovery. Nope. Wrong. Take cover. Don't slide into self-righteous superiority and spiritual smugness. Humility provides the bombproof coverage you need to stay focused and avoid your ego's explosives.

Another potential pitfall to anticipate emerges from your natural human instincts. God designed us with survival instincts to avoid danger and stay alive. These include security and safety, food and drink, love and sex, shelter and warmth, rest and sleep, esteem and approval, and mastery and control. You can't separate these powerful intrinsic instincts from yourself as a person—and you shouldn't try. After all, they help keep you alive by regulating your body, ensuring you eat and drink, get rest and sleep, avoid life-threatening situations, and do the work necessary to keep going.

The problem is that your instincts can expand until they're ironically impeding their intended purpose. For example, your need for relationships include companionship, friendship, affection, erotic love, and so on. If you fixate on these, however, you suddenly set yourself up for people pleasing, passive-aggressive relating, and sex and love addiction. Or, if your instinct for love gets stuck in the groove of attraction to unhealthy individuals who reenact past trauma and abuse, you can get stuck in ways that might destroy your life. Or, if you fear abandonment and being alone too much, you might get clingy and codependent, smothering someone until you drive that person away and enact your own self-fulfilling expectation. Your instincts are divine gifts, but keep an eye on how they can become your center of attention.

Other possible challenges with Step Six revolve around your attempts to once again do God's job for him. You might think you know what order you should begin eliminating defective habits in order to replace them with constructive spiritual practices . . . only to discover that you can't do it. Perhaps you will try to channel all your excitement and enthusiasm into a quicker pace for healing and recovery. Suddenly, you're impatient and frustrated and wondering why God's not doing anything . . . only to discover you're in his way.

You will likely face the temptation to think you're smarter than the average bear and so special that you're the exception to what millions of others have done in working the Steps. So you decide to cut corners and look for hacks and shortcuts. Nope, the path of recovery requires a slow and steady pace of following your Higher Power, not racing ahead.

- Where has your ego been setting booby traps as you engage with working Step Six? How are you learning to discern between your ego's attempts to control change versus God's presence in transforming you?

- Which of your instincts have tended to veer out of control and inflate into addiction and compulsive behaviors? What have you learned from trying to control these tendencies in the past? (This challenge can be especially difficult because your instincts cannot be separated from your humanity. You need food, but no longer overeating requires relating to your body's appetite for food in new and different ways. Your sexuality is inherent to being human, but to stop looking at porn necessitates a fresh perspective on your body, gender identity, and sexuality.)

- What thoughts and feelings stir inside you as you anticipate God removing your character defects (defenses) as an ongoing, lifelong process? What practices and truths can you use to cultivate patience?

- What do you consider to be your greatest personal challenges to anticipate, avoid, or prevent as you work through Step Six? What tactics can you employ to be "entirely ready" for them when they show up?

CONNECTING WITH OTHERS

Working Step Six, you should accept that most of your character defects (your defenses) will not instantly disappear. Some might, which is miraculous and wonderful, but that's not what the majority of people working the Steps experience. Most will tell you that recovery remains a lifelong learning process and an ongoing journey toward greater health, healing, and happiness.

Perhaps it might help you accept the process more patiently if you realize how long these defects have had to take root, blossom, and yield their bitter harvest in your neural pathways. Because one of the key aspects of being entirely ready for God to take them is accepting his timetable. You're no longer in charge of making it happen, so why bother trying to speed up the process? God decides which defects he will remove, the right time for their removal, and his method for removing them. Have faith that he's doing all those things and more, whether you can sense evidence of his divine process or not.

While you might not realize it initially, connecting with others is essential to working Step Six. The language specifies you being entirely ready to let go and let God take them from you. But how does God do this? How do you experience Divine Love in your life on a daily basis? How do you realize real change is taking place?

Most frequently, through other people.

You will continually need their support to reassure you, their encouragement to uplift you, and their honest observations about what they see God doing in your life. After your success with being crazy vulnerable in confessing to someone in Step Five, you've realized that *you're worth loving* despite your brokenness. Remember to welcome others into the process as you discover that not only can you express your emotional needs in healthy ways but you can also offer them a glimpse of where you see God working in them.

* What's necessary for you to find the sweet spot between actively letting go of your character defects without allowing your ego to grab the wheel? What attitude or mindset can you cultivate to remain grounded in this zone?

* What are some ways you've experienced God at work in your recovery through other people? While you might expect to glimpse your Greater Power when relating to your sponsor, your confessor from Step Five, or others in recovery, when was the last time you unexpectedly encountered someone reflecting the Divine?

• Who are the people you rely on most for support, encouragement, prayer, and accountability in your recovery journey? Name at least three of them below. How does each relationship facilitate your ongoing spiritual awakening?

Person	How this relationships facilitates spiritual awakening

• Other than your sponsor, who can you ask for regular reality checks about your spiritual growth? Consider keeping a regular time and place to meet or way to communicate so this person can give you honest feedback on how he or she sees God is changing you—as well as any blind spots covering defects that you need to hand over. Fill out the following:

Who you will ask? _____

Where, when, and how often you will meet? _____

_____

What method you will use to communicate regularly? _____

_____

For the next session: Reread chapter 8, "Okay, I'm Willing Already," in *The Fix*, this time paying closer attention to comparing and contrasting Steps Six and Seven. Consider how they work together in tandem as well how they are distinct from one another. If you're participating in a group study, be prepared to share a summary of your findings.

7

SURRENDER THE SHORTCOMINGS

STEP SEVEN: Humbly asked Him to remove our shortcomings.

Steps Six and Seven are like the StairMaster of the Twelve Steps.

Just in case you were tempted to think being "entirely ready" to have your Higher Power remove your "defects of character" was too easy, Step Seven makes sure you know who is ultimately responsible for their removal. Steps Six and Seven sound similar, but they're distinct. I chose to explore them together in chapter 8, "Okay, I'm Willing Already," in *The Fix*. We can make some slight distinctions, which we'll get to momentarily, but first let's think of them as a complementary couple.

If you got the ball rolling in Step Six, then with Seven you realize you're moving forward in a kind of gyre or spiral instead of a straight line. Sure, it would be great to work Step Six and just keep going without looking back. You've gathered by now, however, that the Twelve Steps are not about mastery as much as mystery, not about perfection as much as progress. Step Six shifts us into an openhearted, mindful attitude of considering our character defects (or defenses, as I see them, you'll recall) and being prepared to release them to God. Step Seven keeps the momentum by humbly asking him to remove them. These two Steps work together, over and over again, facilitating the ongoing spiritual shift that's started in you.

Where Step Six pivots on being "entirely ready," Step Seven spotlights "humbly asking"—the love child of humility and curiosity. These two virtues are part of getting ready to release the storage units of baggage you've been dragging around, but they take you beyond preparation directly to the launching pad. Humility requires you to shift your gaze from your own navel and focus on other people—and not so you can point out the specks in their eyes. No, true humility recognizes the planks in our own eyes but responds with compassion, gentleness, and vulnerability. The humility required to work Step Seven not only acknowledges you cannot change by your own power but also invites you to ask for help from the only One who can.

While they may share some linguistic genealogy, humility is not about its cousin, humiliation. They share an emphasis on powerlessness with a crucial difference: humiliation involves an embarrassing exposure of your weaknesses, failures, character defects, and shortcomings, while humility invites you to acknowledge them yourself. Rather than working to perpetuate a cover-up of the darkness in your shadow, humility flips on the soft glow—not the harsh blue-white LED light of a police interrogation—so you can see into your shadow side.

In order to wave goodbye to your character defects and shortcomings, however, you have to let go. You've likely heard the various jokes about people waiting to be rescued during a hurricane / flood / tornado / tsunami / Black Friday sale who missed the life preserver in front of them because they refuse to let go of past debris. They would rather cling to the familiar and try to walk in the old cement blocks encasing their feet than ask God to dissolve those weights so they could skip into freedom.

Step Seven, however, draws your attention to the fact that acknowledging your own powerlessness and need for divine help is the only key for liberation. But it's a key you will have to leave in the lock and turn again and again—because even after you begin stepping into freedom, you may be tempted to run back to the comfy, familiar incarceration of your addiction. Practicing this seventh Step repeatedly also reinforces the need to practice humility as an ongoing part of your recovery rather than a speed zone temporarily requiring you to take your foot off the pedal. No, my friend, there's no need to hurry up and wait. Working the Steps means your speed of life has forever changed.

- When have you experienced a humiliating situation that set off shame, embarrassment, and guilt inside you? What are some ways your addictions and character defects have caused you to experience humiliation?

- By contrast with humiliation, how would you define and describe humility? When have you felt humbled without shame or embarrassment?

- As you understand Steps Six and Seven, how do you distinguish between "defects of character" and "shortcomings"? If we do *not* assume they're synonymous, how might they differ in illuminating distinct aspects of who you are?

- Based on your experience, how do you practice true humility and not just humble bragging? What tends to tilt you toward humility rather than your own image, willpower, or efforts?

MEETING YOU WHERE YOU ARE

Step Seven reminds you that self-compassion is essential in order to persevere on your Twelve Steps recovery journey. Your fears, both conscious and unconscious, usually activate your character defenses and showcase your shortcomings. This is why doing your fear inventory is so important! Without knowing the underlying fears supporting the defenses they manifest, you're basically pulling weeds without getting the roots.

To overcome your defects of character and shortcomings, you must realize you can't uproot them yourself. Rather than blaming yourself for this universal aspect of your humanity, you must be honest as well as gracious with yourself. Rather than solar-stare directly at the truth of who you are, view yourself through the protective lenses of compassion, acceptance, and curiosity.

Which brings us to considering whether there are any differences between a character defect and a shortcoming. Again, they're often used interchangeably in recovery, yet I wonder if they're providing different angles of the same problem. Defects of character remind me of those trees you've seen that have twisted and bent from the severe winds and storms they've endured. They continued to grow, but they had to adapt to the challenges thrown at them. Shortcomings, on the other hand, usually refer to . . . well, falling short of the mark, not up to the standard expected, required, or set by yourself, others, the church, social media, or some other aspect of culture.

For example, if you almost always feel activated by anger, frustration, and powerlessness any time you have to wait or wait longer than expected, then you're short on patience. If you feel like the exception to obeying rules and guidelines set by authorities (those laws and requirements are good for others, but you don't need them or have to follow them), then you lack the moral and ethical fortitude that considers the needs of others and society as a whole. Whether we call such deficits character defects (defenses) or shortcomings, the key is to learn how they contribute to who you are and how you've lived with your addictions. Regardless of what you call them, the most important thing is to become a lifelong student of yourself.

As you grow in your awareness of your frailties and flaws, don't shame yourself, which often ignites the fuse of trying harder. Fixating and ruminating on your imperfections is not the path forward. Berating yourself while you're down for having your particular mixed cocktail of character defects is just adding one more character defect to the blend! Remember, you've developed these defects and shortcomings as defenses and survival strategies. You've done what you had to do in your life to survive.

But what once helped you survive is now blocking your path. You no longer think of those addictive, defensive strategies because they've become part of your default operating system. In order to unplug them as your automatic go-to, you have to cultivate self-awareness (thus, the many parts of your inventory) as well as an understanding of the connections between those parts of you and your unhealthy habits and unwanted behaviors. Shaming and blaming yourself only creates a loop that reinforces the old system. Understanding, accepting, and being kind to yourself creates new neuropathways in your brain, allowing for changes in how you think, feel, and act. Every time you work Step Seven (which, of course, follows Six), you're evolving into freedom and becoming a better you.

- Do you more frequently tilt toward excuses, entitlement, and indulgence when stressed/activated or toward shame, contempt, and self-contempt? What past situations, events, relationships, and traumas have contributed to the default system you usually follow?

- What are some ways you can cultivate self-awareness and self-compassion as you work through Step Six and Step Seven? What do you need to remember when you're tempted to shame and blame yourself in the face of your defects and shortcomings?

- While a comprehensive, seemingly endless list of defects and shortcomings can be overwhelming, it's still helpful to keep a running list as you become more self-aware and work Steps Six and Seven repeatedly. For now, list your top ten defects of character and shortcomings. (You can reference the list of Character Defects in appendix G if you have trouble coming up with ten.)

1. _____

2. _____

3. _____

4. _____

5. _____

6. _____

7. _____

8. _____

9. _____

10. _____

MOVING FORWARD

As you work Steps Six and Seven (and continue working them), you'll discover various tools and resources that can help you shift your perspective and see some of the character defenses that have gone unnoticed because of your ego's blindfold. If you know much about me at all, you know that the Enneagram is one of my favorite resources for learning more about myself, other people, the mystery of the human personality, and spiritual transformation.

Basically, the Enneagram reveals nine types, with each linking to aspects of other types depending on different variables. Each Enneagram type reveals an umbrella of shortcomings and character defects, which operate and overlap into other types. For example, I'm an Enneagram Four, which often has envy supporting my umbrella of vices, but I occasionally battle with perfectionism, a hallmark characteristic of Ones. You can find more about each type in chapter 8 of *The Fix* as well as at my website (ianmorgancron.com) and podcast (typology-podcast.com), but for your convenience, here's an overview to help you respond to the questions that follow. Remember, the focus is on learning more about how you operate and why you operate that way as you let go of self-improvement and embrace spiritual growth.

Enneagram Ones—Anger, resentment, fear of change, perfectionism, closed-mindedness, control, dualistic thinking, impatience, intolerance, judgmentalism, superiority/inferiority, legalistic, hypocritical, rigidity, defensiveness, deflecting blame, needing to be right, self-righteousness, an unforgiving spirit, overactive inner critic, condescending, patronizing, dogmatic, belief that their way is the only correct way, preachy.

Enneagram Twos—Pride, codependency, overly focused on the needs of others, disavowing their own feelings and needs, assuming they know the needs of others better than they actually do, controlling behavior, manipulation, resentment, expecting others to know and meet their needs without having to acknowledge them, pretending to like people that they don't, self-pity, detachment, isolating, refusing to receive gifts and compliments, believing they're not worthy of love.

Enneagram Threes—Deceit, image management, narcissistic behavior, insincerity, posturing, focusing more on externals than internals, over-valuing success and the admiration of others, chameleonlike behavior, cutting corners to ensure success, workaholism, accumulating status symbols, self-marketing, self-deceit, insincerity, gaslighting, manipulating others, viewing relationships as expendable, playing to the room, performing feelings rather than having feelings, embellishing achievements, boastful, too socially and professionally competitive, vanity.

Enneagram Fours—Envy, self-absorption, overidentifying with feelings, jealousy, perfectionism, focusing on an idealized past and future, fixing attention on what's missing, taking things personally, ingratitude, melancholic, moody, volatile, overly dependent or codependent, misunderstood, isolating, self-harming behaviors, unstable relationships, elitism, dependency, believing they're special and unique, fantasizing, self-pity, superior, ungrateful, comparing self to others.

Enneagram Fives—Avarice, hoarding time and material resources, privacy and personal autonomy, emotional unavailability, intellectual snobbery, aloof, overfocus on self-sufficiency and independence, entitled, isolating, self-aggrandizement, paranoid, misunderstood, miserliness.

Enneagram Sixes—Fear, future-tripping, dependency on authority figures, indecisiveness, pessimism, paranoia, suspicious, distrusting, anxious, worried, slow to act and/or follow through, catastrophizing, pessimistic, deconstructive, reductive, unwilling to meet their own needs, depressive, self-justifying.

Enneagram Sevens—Gluttony, lack of empathy, overindulging anything pleasurable, overly in pursuit of new experiences and stimulation, fear of suffering and painful feelings, difficulty remaining in the present moment, tendency toward addictive behaviors, dishonesty, reframing, rationalizing questionable behaviors and decisions, self-justification, impulsive, self-important, thrill-seeking, promise-breaking.

Enneagram Eights—Lust, controlling others and the environment to mask vulnerability, combativeness, domineering, intimidation, impulsive decision-making, overly autocratic, making rules for others while breaking them, legalistic, vengeful, difficulty apologizing, dismissing those who aren't as strong as they are, oppositional, obstructive, sarcastic, excessive.

Enneagram Nines—Sloth, laziness, shortsighted and missing the bigger picture, brokering peace at any cost, indecisive, merging with the agenda of groups and individuals, self-abandonment and self-negation, distractibility, dependency, codependency, passive-aggressive anger, stubbornness, dishonesty when stressed, apathetic, failure to self-invest, conflict-avoidant, forgetful, lack of purpose, procrastination, denying anger, resisting growth.

- What tools and resources have you used previously to become more self-aware of your defects and shortcomings? How did they provide fresh insights on how and why you struggle with addiction?

- Whether the Enneagram is new to you or you've been studying it for decades, how can it facilitate your work with Step Six and Step Seven? Which facets of yourself does it help you see with greater clarity?

- If you're familiar with the Enneagram, you know it also reveals the special super-power of each type as well as practices that can address your defects and short-comings. Assuming you know your type (or have some idea of it), what practices will help you grow in self-awareness and humility? How can becoming more aware of your various defects and shortcomings be considered a gift?

- What changes in character would you like to see as a result of working through Step Seven? What will it look like as your Greater Power removes your defects of character and shortcomings?

- What tools and resources do you want to explore and practice more thoroughly? How can they provide support for working Step Six and Step Seven?

CONNECTING WITH OTHERS

While self-awareness and self-compassion are essential to doing Step Seven, you still need community and connections with trusted others to help you keep perspective and remain accountable. Virtually all the tools and resources you find helpful individually can be shared in a group setting. I'm thinking specifically of *prayer* and *meditation*. While these are inherently personal and individual communications between you and your Higher Power, they also provide exponential relational benefits when practiced with others. There's something crazy comforting about sharing your fears, burdens, weaknesses, and defects with others and having them pray for you—even as you listen and pray for them.

You'll find that working Step Six and Step Seven requires confessing and connecting with others in recovery. Looking inward with a hyperfocus can quickly spark into being hypercritical, but participating in what I like to call a "Me, Too" group will remind you that you're not the only one with dark secrets, wrongful behaviors, and warped character defects. These groups are often best if kept smaller, with perhaps only four or five participants, and when everyone willingly commits to rigorous honesty (about themselves and the other participants). These groups need consistency as well—regular ways to check in frequently as well as reliable meeting times and places. In the safety of these small groups, you can share at your most raw and vulnerable level, knowing you will not be judged and trusting you will be accepted and loved.

Keep in mind, working the Steps is a process, which is especially true for Six and Seven. Don't be discouraged if you seem to continue working on some of the same defects and shortcomings for years—heck, for the rest of your life—without seeing their dramatic removal the way you would like. Trust instead that you're growing incrementally and cumulatively as God baby-steps you away from those old systems and leads you into new, life-giving practices. Bill W. emphasized that the Steps are "guides to progress" rather than "spiritual perfection." When you're struggling to sense change, connecting with others will help remind you of why you are working the Steps while pointing out what you may not have noticed in your own spiritual development.

- If you're not presently in a Me, Too group, think through the people in recovery whom you know best and trust most. Choose two or three of them to query about forming a joint effort as you work through Step Six and Step Seven. Figure out the best regular in-person meeting place and time, the frequency of meetings, and ongoing (daily?) check-ins.

Who I would want to have in a Me, Too group:

Two or three people I will query about their interest:

When and where we will meet to discuss next steps:

- Which of my personal examples from chapter 8 in *The Fix* resonates or stands out the most for you? What does this example reveal about the process of working through Steps Six and Seven?

- As you get entirely ready to relinquish your character defects and shortcomings to God (as you understand him), what do you expect from his involvement? What would you like your Greater Power to do in response—other than magically remove every problem area at once?

- Which of your defects of character or shortcomings do you struggle the most to surrender? Why? What benefits do you think these defects have produced to help you cope with life?

- What prayer, affirmation, mantra, adage, proverb, or intention do you want to create and use as you continue working Step Six and Step Seven? Keep it concise (no more than a sentence or two) and try to make it original (okay to borrow from others but make it uniquely your own). Write it below:

For the next session: Read or review chapter 9, "Mea Culpa," in *The Fix*. If you're participating in a group study, choose one character defect or shortcoming you've uncovered and explored while working Step Seven to share at your next meeting.

8

LIST THOSE HARMED

STEP EIGHT: Made a list of all persons we had harmed, and became willing to make amends to them all.

Ah, Step Eight . . .

Working Steps Six and Seven may have turned out to be harder than you expected, in part because their work, like that of all the Steps, is ongoing. You might be feeling a little Step fatigue—a bit of recovery vertigo as you consider how far you've come. That's understandable, and if you need to take a break and pace yourself, feel free to do so. Just be intentional and set a deadline for when you will move on from Step Seven to Step Eight rather than procrastinate and put it off because you've heard that Step Eight will require so much of you.

So, first, the bad news. What you've heard about Step Eight is correct, my friend. If you expected to pick up speed as you progressed through the Twelve Steps and arrive at your recovery summit in record time, that's not how it works. (If this is what you are thinking, then Step Eight will not be a speed bump but a serious obstacle.) Rather, it's all about process, progress, and perseverance. The moment you claim you've arrived—regardless of how many years of sobriety you have—you're going to lose your grip and slide down the mountainside. After you scale the peak of one Step and reach a plateau, you climb the next.

And the good news? Step Eight and Step Nine invite you to make a giant stride toward freedom, happiness, and a sense of lightness and peace that you've never experienced. Once you complete Step Eight, your life—and the lives of most of the people you know and care about—will become a lot more enjoyable. This is because you probably don't realize how much the guilt and shame of hurting others has been weighing on you.

So, Step Eight now invites you to switch to a shame-free, guilt-free relational diet. All of us born into this world suffer both the wounds that others inflict on us, through both omission and commission, as well as the pain we experience from injuring others. In order to address our fears, our identity, our worth, and our purpose, we must now take responsibility for our own actions and be willing to make amends. Step Nine complements and builds from Eight (similar to Steps Six and Seven), so we'll explore what making amends is all about in the next session. Step Eight only asks that you make your list of people you've harmed and be willing to make amends for the injury you've inflicted.

Here's the kicker: In order to take responsibility for the impact of harming others, you will have to forgive yourself and those who have harmed you as well. Whether you call it karma, space for grace, or forgiving those who have trespassed against you so you have capacity to be forgiven, they're all in the same jewelry-box drawer of old chains and necklaces knotted together.

The process may seem just as tedious and time-consuming as untangling those strands, but it's more than worth it. When you've worked through Step Eight, you will be halfway down the road to freedom from the burden of shame, guilt, regret, fear, sadness, anger, and resentment that's crushing your soul. This eighth Step requires a muscle-stretching leap because it closes the gap separating you from God, yourself, and others. While you may always experience some distance within that gap, I'm sure you'll agree there's a big difference between bridging San Francisco Bay and a mountain stream.

If you've worked Steps One through Seven, then you've established the scaffolding necessary to traverse Step Eight. You've probably noticed that Steps One through Three focus on healing your relationship with God while Steps Four through Seven require mending your relationship with yourself. You're now ready to work on repairing relationships with other people. Steps Eight and Nine facilitate how to clear the wreckage from your past along with the collateral damage of your addictions.

- How would you describe the process of working through the Twelve Steps up to this point? What comparison or metaphor best describes your experience as you now move into Step Eight?

- What are some of the ways you've harmed other people in the past? Check all that apply and add others that come to mind:

  - ☐ lying and deception (overtly and by omission)
  - ☐ betrayal
  - ☐ cheating/stealing
  - ☐ spiteful and harsh words
  - ☐ violence
  - ☐ harmful thoughts and attitudes
  - ☐ humiliation
  - ☐ rejection and abandonment
  - ☐ isolating and pushing others away
  - ☐ self-pity
  - ☐ entitlement and justification
  - ☐ other ways:

- What do you see as the potential benefits of taking ownership for the ways you've harmed others? How does what you will gain with Step Eight motivate you to keep up the hard work and patient persistence necessary to work the Steps?

- How have you usually responded to an awareness of causing harm to others in the past? Do you tilt toward being a villainized victim or a misunderstood martyr? Something else? Explain your response.

MEETING YOU WHERE YOU ARE

We all long to receive acknowledgment of wrongdoing accompanied by a sincere request for forgiveness from those who have hurt us. Whether we want a parent to validate the harm they did when we were a preschooler or hope for an apology from a coworker who "mistakenly" ate our lunch in the breakroom, we know how powerful a simple "I'm sorry" or "Please forgive me" can be.

You likely have people who have hurt you who have never acknowledged the pain they caused you. As you begin the intimidating process of taking responsibility for the harm you've caused, just consider how your life might be better if those perpetrators of your pain had owned up and asked what you needed in order to forgive them. In other words, working Step Eight is focused on giving this gift to others, but in so doing, you're also gifting yourself.

The process begins by simply brainstorming a list of those whom you know you've hurt. Yes, I'm well aware of how misleading that sounds, as if you're updating your vacation bucket list or jotting down what you need from the grocery store. You will likely have a handful of obvious candidates, particularly family members—parents, siblings, your spouse or partner, and your children. Even with those relationships, though, try to be as specific as you can in recalling how you've harmed them. Not simply, "I lied to my spouse," but, "Oh, yeah, that time last summer when I lied about why I came home late that night . . . and had to keep lying to cover my tracks."

Why be so specific? Because your Teflon-coated ego loves to shuck and jive to avoid taking responsibility for the damage you've caused. So if you find yourself procrastinating and stalling out with composing your list, or if you keep getting hung up on how comprehensively to define *harm*, then check your ego. There's a good chance the fast-talking, slow-moving prisoner is trying to escape the power of the truth.

If you're not sure what qualifies as harm, simply write down anything done or said to you that made *you* feel angry, resentful, hurt, ashamed, sad, or afraid—and then quickly follow with the names of the people you have hurt by doing those very same things. In the midst of working Step Eight and writing your list of those you've harmed, you might begin explaining away certain incidents, questioning if real harm was done due to the context. Because, obviously, what that person did to you was far worse than what you did in return, right?

Sorry, but Step Eight keeps the spotlight on you—not on those who harmed you. Yes, you will likely think about all the wounds and wrongs done to you as you work through this Step. But don't lose the purposeful plot of this twist in your story—you're concentrating on ownership of your part without any excuses, qualifications, or caveats. This is not about dragging in evidence to exonerate yourself. Step Eight is about taking a long, hard look at your own misdeeds and misdemeanors.

- Who are some of the people in your past who hurt you without ever acknowledging their harm or asking for your forgiveness? What difference would it have made at the time if they had apologized and made amends? What difference would it make if they were to do so now?

- Look back at the items you checked in response to the ways you've harmed others in the past (and any others that you added). Choose one of the categories that has contributed to a recurring pattern of harming others in your life and describe a couple of specific examples (perhaps one from years ago and another that's recent). For example, you might choose "humiliation" as the category and then describe the time you humiliated your sister when you were in high school as well as the way you humiliated your coworker during last week's meeting.

Category: _____

Past example:	Recent example:

- Where do you see connections between the kinds of harm you've experienced and the kinds of harm you've inflicted on others? How does the way you harm others perpetuate or reenact what was done to you in the past?

- What explanations and excuses have you used to justify some of the harm you've caused others? Who has harmed you and then experienced similar or worse harm from you in return?

MOVING FORWARD

You might be tempted to combine Step Eight and Step Nine into a giant staircase that seems impossible to climb. While these Steps do work together in healing you, others, and your relationships, they are separate and distinct Steps for a reason. If you conflate them and focus only on the outcome and not how you got there, then you'll probably feel overwhelmed, intimidated, and too ashamed to get started. When you jump from putting a name on your list to imagining the cringeworthy conversation that will be required to admit hurting that person and making amends, you bite off more than most people can chew.

This is why Step Eight only asks you to focus on two parts: (1) making your list, and (2) being willing to made amends. Granted, these two pieces of Step Eight are moving you in an action-oriented direction, but not all at once. All that's required as you work through Step Eight is to make a list of people you know you've hurt and become accountable enough to want to make it up to them. Nothing further is required. You can take a deep, emotional breath before lifting the curtain to consider how to work Step Nine.

So don't engage in casting calls and dress rehearsals in your mind that are filled with previously unimaginable conversations with equally uncomfortable people. It's easy to start future-tripping into how you envision your brother will respond when you confess that horrible thing you said to him at Christmas last year. You know what you would then want to say in return and how the historical dynamics between the two of you would suddenly hijack your attempt to take responsibility and make amends.

You might think that if you can't defend yourself in such a confessional conversation, then it will turn into an invitation for people like your brother to heap on and kick you while you're down. We'll go over how to prepare for actual conversations and attempts at making amends in the next session with Step Nine. For now, try to let go of imagining all the things that *might* happen.

Remember, too, that you're not alone and not working Step Eight in your own power. So enlist spiritual support through prayer, meditation, and community with trusted others. In fact, before you even *start* your list, spend some time in prayer. Ask God (as you know him) to help you remember the individuals you have harmed in some way during your life. Pray for strength and courage to face all the ways—physically, emotionally, mentally, spiritually, professionally, sexually, and/or financially—that you've harmed others.

Don't stop to try and measure or compare the ways you've harmed people. Whether it's a big, obvious elephant in the room or a small, subtle mouse, just list the person and move on. There's no expiration date or statute of limitations, so cover the expanse of your memory from earliest to earlier today. Remember, right now you're just listing names and opening the eyes of your heart to see the impact of what you did.

- What thoughts and feelings challenge your ability to make your list of people you've harmed? How can you keep the focus on identifying these people and acknowledging you harmed them without allowing your imagination to jump ahead?

- Why does reconciling with your Higher Power also require reconciling with the people you've harmed? How is forgiveness a spiritual endeavor?

- What character defects and shortcomings have prevented you from owning responsibility and being willing to make amends up until now?

- How does forgiving those who have harmed you empower you to take responsibility for harming others and making amends? What have you learned from those you have forgiven that you can now apply to yourself?

CONNECTING WITH OTHERS

Step Eight requires you to connect with others in order to facilitate healing—for them and for you. And you can safely assume that making your list will stir up all kinds of painful memories, shameful regrets, and anxious uncertainty. As excruciating as it may be, you have to feel the weight of how you've hurt others—or you won't change. You must experience a sense of what other people felt when you harmed them and take ownership of it. Otherwise, you will continue to leave room for your ego to justify, excuse, explain, and escape. Your addictions once helped you numb painful feelings and dodge responsibility, and now you can weaken their hold on you by staring through the eyes of your shadow as you gaze at the suffering you've caused others to experience.

So let's get down to the nitty-gritty, shall we? To help you with your list and to soften your heart toward the harm you've caused, fill in the following. Feel free to use this template in your journal or another format in order to facilitate completing Step Eight and preparing yourself for Step Nine.

Who I harmed: _____ Contact information: _____
How I harmed him/her: _____
Why I did what I did: _____
How I feel about it now: _____
Specific amends to restore relationship: _____
_____

Who I harmed: _____ Contact information: _____
How I harmed him/her: _____
Why I did what I did: _____
How I feel about it now: _____
Specific amends to restore relationship: _____

_____

Who I harmed: _____ Contact information: _____
How I harmed him/her: _____
Why I did what I did: _____
How I feel about it now: _____
Specific amends to restore relationship: _____

_____

Who I harmed: _____ Contact information: _____
How I harmed him/her: _____
Why I did what I did: _____
How I feel about it now: _____
Specific amends to restore relationship: _____

_____

Who I harmed: _____ Contact information: _____
How I harmed him/her: _____
Why I did what I did: _____
How I feel about it now: _____
Specific amends to restore relationship: _____

_____

For the next session: Before moving on, reread chapter 9, "Mea Culpa," in *The Fix*. Focus your attention on stepping from Step Eight into Step Nine as you consider acting to make amends on what you've uncovered. If you are participating in a group study, share one challenge or struggle you're facing in completing Steps Eight and Nine to share at your next meeting.

9

MAKE AMENDS

STEP NINE: Made direct amends to such people wherever possible, except when to do so would injure them or others.

Your shift from Step Eight into Step Nine will rarely glide smoothly and never perfectly. No, this shift is much more like the manual transmission in an old Jeep Wrangler that I once took for a test-drive. The seller had told me that once I moved beyond second gear, "she runs a little rough." I'd nodded like it was no big deal. Like I was a weathered stunt driver known as the Jeep-Whisperer who could coax any engine into full-throttled compliance.

Wrong.

Shifting the stick of that "classic" Wrangler into third gear was like trying to thread a needle with a ten-pound dumbbell. I knew if I bought the old beast that I would soon have the strongest right arm imaginable, because it was more than a workout. Practically speaking, it would have been hugely frustrating to be in a hurry or assume I could arrive at my destination on time.

Completing Step Nine might leave you feeling the same way if you're hoping for a leisurely drive up the coastal highway. Doing the ninth Step takes time and may move you along in fits and starts. The process will require more prayer, and some sweat and tears, as you follow through on the hard work of Step Eight and make direct amends wherever possible.

And there are a number of reasons as to why it might *not* be possible. Step Nine recognizes this scenario with an important caveat. You are to make direct amends to the people on your list whom you've harmed "except when to do so would injure them or others." In other words, you don't want to compound the harm you've already inflicted by attempting to make amends that result in greater distress for the person you hurt.

The "wherever possible" phrase that is included in Step Nine also recognizes other obstacles, including those that are self-imposed and require time (and spiritual growth) to dislodge. Bill W. knew better than to presume that once people completed their list in Step Eight that they would be giddy with anticipation about making amends to everyone on it. He knew that they would most likely have some personal work to do before they were able to have the necessary hard conversations and make the even harder amends.

You see, some people on your list will be much easier to approach and offer amends to than others. Some of those people whom you've harmed will stand out to you because you know they didn't deserve what you did to them—how you lied and cheated and betrayed them, or whatever other harm that you inflicted. It's still painful, but you must be willing to own it and do all you can to offer whatever you can to make things better, both for them as well as for your relationship (assuming they still want a relationship with you).

You've probably already noticed, however, that other people on your list will trigger you into a seething mess of emotional pain and angry retribution. Make amends to those people who treated you like that and did that to you? Are you kidding me? No _____ way (you can fill in your own choice for emphasis here, my friend).

These people you struggle to approach, apologize, and makes amends with often end up on a shorter list (well, at least I hope yours is shorter) by necessity. The way that I think about my list of these people reflects my contempt for them and reveals the problem. Whatever you call your short list of tough nuts to crack, just recognize that you're going to have to forgive them before you can move on and own how you've hurt them.

It's okay to not be where you need to be to make amends as long as you're willing to do what's necessary to move in that direction. As you work on forgiving them, you realize that you're *being willing* (shout out to Step Eight) to do what's required in order to move forward with Step Nine. Rather than getting stuck in any grudges, you can follow the wisdom Bill W. offers in *The Big Book*: "If we haven't the will to do this, we ask until it comes."[5]

- What aspects of working the Steps have you found to be especially challenging so far? What has motivated you to persevere and continue to do your work?

- Who are the people on your list from Step Eight to whom you're ready to offer an apology and make amends? Why does the process of making amends to them seem more straightforward and less complicated than some of the others?

- Who are those people on your list who have harmed *you*? What makes offering amends to these individuals incredibly difficult if not impossible? What feelings rise up in you as you consider your resistance to making amends with them?

- What do you need to do in order to move in the direction toward forgiving them? What's one step you can take toward repairing the rupture in your relationship with these people who have hurt you?

MEETING YOU WHERE YOU ARE

By the time you reach Step Nine, you're likely ready for action. If you've made it this far through the Steps, you're clearly serious about your recovery, and you know what's required of you—mostly surrendering control and pursuing spiritual practices. You've focused on getting acquainted with your Higher Power and cultivating a deeper relationship. You've started working on your relationship with yourself (a lifelong endeavor if ever there was one). Now you're doing what probably feels like the hardest work possible. You're not merely working on improving your relationships—you're owning up and paying back.

Once you've finished your list, you and your sponsor (or your sponsor-type-trusted-surrogate) can go over it and discern whether every name belongs on there. You may recognize that some of the ways you hurt someone else seem huge to you but might have gone unnoticed by them. For instance, maybe you've felt guilty all these years for TP'ing your high school biology teacher's house, but now, decades later, he's retired and lives in Florida. Sure, it's important to acknowledge before God, to yourself, and to your sponsor that you hurt him, but you can probably let that one go and move on.

Step Nine asks you to follow through with your overall intention of working the Steps. You not only want a better life that is free of the vise-grip of your addictions and compulsive behaviors, but you also want to become truly useful to God and to serve others. One of the best ways to accomplish this significant intention is to reconcile with the people you've harmed and make amends for the suffering you've caused. Doing what you can to restore relationships and make things right also frees you from the chains of guilt, shame, and self-contempt that are weighing you down.

Finally, keep in mind the word *amend* basically means to add something in order to improve it, complete it, restore it, and make it better. You cannot undo the past damage you've caused, but you can acknowledge it and try to do what's necessary to reset. I once heard a retired contractor describe Steps Eight and Nine as a process of assessing the damage you caused in your former days as a hurricane. In the throes of your addiction, you wreaked havoc and wrecked lives—your own as well as others. Now, like a good insurance claims adjuster, you're going back to see the damage you did and offering restoration.

But the process requires continuing to grow in humility, faith, and self-compassion. These are the building blocks that the God of your understanding uses to rebuild the relationships you damaged. Because all the work you've done might be helpful, but it won't stick unless you get rid of the rot and replace it with solid support. Making amends means it's time to roll up your sleeves, take action, and let others experience some of the ways you're changing.

- Which names did you, with some help from your sponsor, cull from your list? What are the reasons for not moving forward in making amends to them?

- What does "direct amends" mean to you? Why is your attitude of willingness not enough to move forward?

- How does making amends specifically benefit the people you've harmed? How does making amends specifically benefit you and your recovery?

- What do you need from your Higher Power in order take action and make amends? How can prayers, affirmations, meditations, and spiritual practices provide the support you need to do what feels unbearable at times?

MOVING FORWARD

You know from personal experience that there's a right way and a wrong way to ask for forgiveness and make amends. You understand the difference because you've been on the receiving side of half-hearted, insincere, going-through-the-motions apologies that resulted in disappointment and further resentment. You have received a gift, favor, or so-called restitution that felt more like the product of a plea bargain than wholehearted, humbly offered amends. So, as you move into having some difficult conversations and making amends, keep in mind your commitment to do more good than harm, move toward restoration rather than explanation, and clear the way forward for others as well as yourself.

While there's no definitive way or perfect formula for making amends, you will find it helpful to keep a few things in mind. While there are several different kinds of amends, the type that is referenced in Step Nine—"direct amends"—remains the best and most effective. Making direct amends involves in-person, real-life engagement and conversation with a person whom you've harmed. To help you facilitate making direct amends, I offer the following tips that have helped me and countless others.

First, *be direct and specific about why you are requesting the meeting*. You should "name it and claim it," fully acknowledging your wrongdoing and expressing your sincere remorse. Respect the other person with kindness, direct eye contact, and body language that reflects your humility, courage, and openness. As painful as it may be, you must show that person your sincerity in owning and regretting the hurt you caused. The other person needs to see you're serious and not dodging the weight of how you wounded them. Don't try to be charming, coy, funny, or anything other than authentic. Make it clear you're willing to experience that person's response and anything he or she cares to say—and that you're *asking* for forgiveness and not assuming it's automatic.

This leads to my second suggestion: *Give the person space to share his or her feelings and thoughts openly and honestly*. This might be the hardest part of your conversation, but you have to hear what the person has to say, including the exact details about how badly he or she has suffered because of what you did, without interruption from you. Don't stop to correct, analyze, question, or clarify—just listen and remain receptive to his or her unvarnished truth.

Be prepared as well for the person to question your motives and the timing of your conversation. You don't have to go into detail about your recovery journey, but at least anticipate letting them know what has prompted you to come forward at this time. In response, you might be tempted to do some damage control and try to soften the edges of the cuts you inflicted. (You know, provide context that reframes what you did and subtly, or not so subtly, try to undermine, minimize, or rationalize the impact of the harm you did.) Don't do this. Remember, you're there to make things better—not stir up the past, offer mixed motives for the present, or create new fodder for the future. So try to offer clarity that keeps the full responsibility with you.

Next, *propose appropriate amends while inviting the person to add anything else he or she wants to say.* Be direct in offering the specific amends you have in mind, and then ask if those amends will be acceptable or if he or she has another idea or something further for you to do. Let the person know you're aware that what you're offering cannot erase the pain or undo the damage you've caused, but make it clear to him or her you want to do something and not just talk about it.

Before you conclude the conversation, *flat out promise to never repeat the harmful actions or offending behavior again.* This is not a polite framing device to wind down your discussion. This promise reinforces the changes taking place within you. Not only are you sorry and want to make amends, but you're also going to be a better human being.

Finally, wrap up your amends convo by *acknowledging that you know you're not perfect but that you're on a spiritual journey to be your best, most authentic self.* You may mess up and even hurt the person again (but not like before), but you will persevere and keep going. You're in pursuit of progress—not perfection!

- When has someone inflicted more harm on you in a botched attempt to apologize or make amends? What did you learn about how to seek forgiveness and make amends that you can carry into your meetings with those you've harmed?

- How would those who know you best describe your verbal communication style? What tendencies do you need to avoid (such as averting your eyes, talking too softly, or joking inappropriately) in order to convey sincerity, respect, and humility when you make amends?

- What criteria will you use in deciding what to offer for making amends? While it's easy to offer to replace an item you've stolen or broken, how will you determine a suitable offering for each person you've harmed?

- What price are you prepared to pay in order to fully make amends to those you've harmed? What will making amends cost you emotionally, physically, mentally, and financially?

CONNECTING WITH OTHERS

Sometimes, no matter how much you may want to make direct amends, you simply can't—at least not the way you desire. People move, and you lose track of where to find them despite your searches on social media. Perhaps it's been decades since you've interacted or communicated with others and you're not even sure if they're still alive. In these cases where you can't have a face-to-face amends conversation, you can make indirect amends.

When you're unable to locate people on your list, you can pray that God will allow your paths to cross at the right time for you to ask for their forgiveness and make amends. You can write them a letter expressing your heartfelt regret over hurting them and describe how you want to make it up to them. While you won't know where to send it, you'll find relief just in expressing most of what you would say in person. You might find similar relief when the person you've harmed is deceased. You can consider taking Step Nine even further by reading your letter where they're buried or in a place that was special to them.

Some of the people on your list might not accept your invitation. They might be so angry, resentful, or unwilling that they refuse to meet or communicate further with you. In these situations, you can continue to pray and hope for opportunities when you might be able to make reparation to them. You can also make part of your amends to them (albeit without their knowledge) by giving, volunteering, or showing kindness in a way that suits that person you've harmed.

Not all relationships will be restored when you make amends, but many will. You may be surprised at how many of your conversations go better than you expect. When others sense you're making a genuine effort to own your past wrongdoing and make restitution, they're often inspired to offer a gracious response. You're not owed that, but receive it when it's offered. A few people may express admiration for your courage and vulnerability and want to support you in recovery. Throughout the process of working Step Nine, Bill W. in *The Big Book* reminds us that ultimately the result is not up to us: "We will suddenly realize that God is doing for us what we could not do for ourselves."[6]

- Who are the people on your list who require some form of indirect amends? List their names below along with at least one way you can make an indirect amend:

Name: _____ Indirect amend: _____

Name: _____ Indirect amend: _____

Name: _____ Indirect amend: _____

Name: _____ Indirect amend: _____

Name: _____ Indirect amend: _____

Name: _____ Indirect amend: _____

- Who do you wish was still alive so that you could make direct amends? How can you express your regret for hurting that person in a way that frees you from guilt, shame, and self-recrimination?

- Which of the people on your list require you to forego direct amends in order not to cause further harm? What's one way you can express your desire to mend the relationship without direct contact with them?

- What has been the most challenging aspect of working Step Nine? How has doing this Step resulted in more peace, compassion, and self-forgiveness?

For the next session: Before moving on to Step Ten, review "Look Out!", chapter 10, in *The Fix*. If you're part of a group study, be prepared to briefly summarize one conversation you've had to make amends since your last group meeting.

10

CONTINUE THE INVENTORY

STEP TEN: Continued to take personal inventory and when we were wrong promptly admitted it.

Brushing and flossing.

Eating more veggies and skipping more desserts.

Scheduling oil changes and tire rotations.

Changing HVAC filters and adjusting thermostats.

Pruning limbs and mulching leaves.

Updating software and deleting spam.

So much of life comes down to maintenance. No matter how many mod-cons, AI programs, and tech systems claim to make our lives easier, ultimately it's still up to us to keep on keeping on. The temptation with maintenance, like so many aspects of life, is to either neglect it and suffer the consequences or become hyper-vigilant and preoccupied with perfection. The goal, as I see it at least, is to practice perseverance toward dynamic growth, not the status quo.

Step Ten reminds you that the same is true for your journey of recovery.

These final three Steps, Ten through Twelve, are often called "maintenance steps" because they help support and sustain your new way of living. The previous nine Steps focused on each of your three most important relationships—with God, with yourself, with other people. Now that you've cleaned house and established order, you can work on growing in these relationships, nurturing your spiritual roots, and enjoying the fruits of recovery.

Step Ten focuses on how you can apply your work in the previous nine Steps to the occupational hazards of daily life. Building on your previous inventories and increased self-awareness, you utilize new tools for better ways of coping than the old default patterns and ruts. You're no longer at the mercy of your past survival strategies with their reactive thoughts, overwhelming emotions, and disruptive behaviors. You're now on a new path forward—a spiritual path leading deeper into wholeness.

As you walk this path using the Twelve Steps, your spiritual sensitivity becomes more attuned to God and his presence that permeates all areas of your life. You become more adept at aligning your thoughts, feelings, choices, and actions with what he wants rather than what your ego thinks it wants. Rather than drifting into previous addictive grooves, you experience a new rhythm.

Sometimes, however, the stress and challenges of life will either disrupt this rhythm or try to silence it. When such ruptures occur, you will be tempted to lose focus and doze off spiritually. You're not the only one to experience such lulls—it's an inherent tendency of humanity. Life provides plenty of distractions, diversions, and disruptions as well, grounding you in the reality of challenges and obstacles that you'd rather not face.

Your addictions provided temporary yet costly relief from those struggles, but now you've found another way to live—one without dependency on other substances and behaviors. You've relinquished control to a loving Greater Power who will continue to guide you even as you adjust to new ways of coping with daily ups and downs. You no longer have to try to exert control or escape the pain. Like the snooze button on your spiritual alarm setting, Step Ten gently reminds you about the gifts of your spiritual awakening. Step Ten reveals that perseverance yields serenity, order, and purpose.

- What situations have activated your anger, fear, and defensive responses in the past? How have you handled such triggers while working the previous Steps?

- In the past, you probably relied on a regular fix to help you function and cope with life's daily challenges. What is currently helping you cope? How are you learning to function in more constructive and responsible ways?

- What are examples of the ways you have recently grown in self-awareness and self-compassion? How has this spiritual growth helped you resist the tendency to slip back into old default patterns of thinking, feeling, and acting?

- When it comes to maintenance chores for your spiritual health or household upkeep, do you tend to procrastinate or stay on top of what needs to be done? What benefits have you experienced from making such maintenance a priority?

MEETING YOU WHERE YOU ARE

Each new day provides opportunities to get in your own way. Life provides enough hard days when everything seems to go wrong—when engines overheat while driving your kids to school, when clients bully you for saying no, when your body aches from the latest viral variant. Like the rest of us, you can't prevent or change those circumstances beyond your control. You can't control what you experience in the moment. But you're not a passive victim of circumstance—you can own your inner landscape and choose how to respond moving forward.

Recognizing your personal responsibility in the midst of unexpected situations and stressful moments requires greater self-awareness as well as new options for what you do with disruptive and unruly thoughts, emotions, and tendencies. This isn't easy, especially when you're used to blaming others, shaming yourself, and using substances or compulsive behaviors to numb uncomfortable feelings. As Bill W. explains, "It is a spiritual axiom that every time we are disturbed, no matter what the cause, there is something wrong with us."[7]

Notice what's going on inside of you in response to that statement. If you're like me, it seems as if the Twelve Steps have a double standard when it comes to how we do life. On the one hand, we're not in control and our addictions have made life unmanageable, which has resulted in us surrendering to our Higher Power. And yet, as we know from the personal inventories in Steps Four and Five, along with the lists of people we've harmed and to whom we're now making amends, we are still responsible for our actions. We're not in control, and yet we're still on the hook. Surely, it's not our fault when things go wrong and we react out of anger, fear, resentfulness, or defensiveness?

Nope, not our fault when things go wrong.

Yep, entirely our responsibility for how we respond.

While we can't avoid life's turbulence, we don't have to be thrown off balance every time something happens. We can own our internal center of gravity and stay grounded. This ability depends largely on the seat of our self-awareness, which operates as a kind of compass for providing self-insight and receiving spiritual guidance. I like to call this new operating system my "Inner Observer," a kind of air traffic controller within my consciousness that helps me land my emotions and get responsible actions off the ground.

Your Inner Observer is definitely not your inner critic—that part of you frequently trying to assess, judge, critique, and shame you no matter what you do or don't do. No, your Inner Observer instead offers perspective, equanimity, and self-encouragement. While listening to your inner critic will immobilize you, listening to your Inner Observer will offer insight and help you regulate your thoughts, feelings, and actions as you go through your day. This part of you steadies your progress as walk through the Steps, gently providing ways to practice good self-governance. It points out when character defects and shortcomings attempt to pull you off-kilter and reminds you of the solid ground of God's power and presence.

Your Inner Observer also tells you when to hit pause before responding and consider what will happen if you give in and act on whatever you're feeling in the moment. This part of you reminds you of better options than acting like a preschooler having a temper tantrum. A crucial part of how your Inner Observer provides feedback is by helping you perform inventories on your behaviors, thoughts, and feelings in real time throughout the day.

- What frustrations and challenges have you experienced in regard to what working the Steps requires of you? How have you handled these thoughts and feelings?

- What recent circumstances and relationships have resulted in unexpected stress, anger, resentment, fear, and uncertainty? How have you handled the temptation to return to using and relying on your addictions and compulsive behaviors?

- How would you describe your inner critic? What name and personality fits the way this voice tries to shame and criticize you?

- How has awareness of your Inner Observer increased since working the Steps? How has your Inner Observer helped you deal with the demands of daily life?

MOVING FORWARD

Your Inner Observer is your greatest ally when it comes to working Step Ten. When you lose touch or ignore your Inner Observer, you will tend to lose perspective and succumb to momentary meltdowns. In order to remain balanced, both being aware of all you're experiencing as well as taking responsibility for how you respond, you will want a new set of personal maintenance tools—also known as daily personal inventories.

These inventories are not busywork to distract you from yourself—just the opposite, in fact. They help you check in with what's going on inside you. Step Ten prompts you to use these inventories to facilitate regular visits with yourself to chart new responses to old triggers. These inventories use an abbreviated or slightly modified version of the personal inventory you learned in Step Four and have built upon until now. The beauty of Step Ten results from its cumulative distillation of Steps Four through Nine all at once.

Like any good multipurpose tool, the personal inventory adapts to help you pause, reflect, and respond at different times and in various situations on any given day. Three of the most basic ways to take a personal inventory include: (1) the mental Spot-Check Inventory, practiced as needed throughout your day; (2) the written Spot-Check Inventory, helpful for externalizing your experience; and (3) the Nightly Inventory, beneficial for more in-depth reflection.

Before you panic and think you're going to be spending the rest of your life filling out personal inventories, keep in mind the value of knowing as much as possible about them in order to adapt and personalize them. I suspect very few people complete all these inventories every single day, but it's good for you to keep them within reach so you can customize this tenth Step to fit your needs and lifestyle.

When someone cuts you off while mouthing expletives as if it's your fault, before you tailgate them and return their unkind gestures, you can do a mental Spot-Check Inventory. When you're waiting more than an hour for your dentist to charge an obscene amount for the privilege of a root canal, instead of losing it and taking out your frustration on the startled-deer receptionist, you can do a mental Spot-Check Inventory. With help from your Inner Observer, the process objectifies what's going on and helps you reconsider your unfiltered reaction. Generally, you hit pause, take a breath, and answer the following questions:

- What am I feeling right now (anger, resentment, frustration)?
- Why am I feeling this way?
- Who am I directing this toward?
- How am I tempted to respond right now?
- What are some better ways that I could respond?
- What's my part in how I'm experiencing this?
- What should I do now?

Let's give it a try. Think of a recent time you were exasperated, frustrated, enraged, annoyed, or aggravated at an intense level. With this particular experience in mind, complete the following inventory to help you absorb the process so you can conduct it on the fly in the moment next time:

When _____

happened, I experienced _____

_____

_____

in the moment because _____

_____

_____ .

I wanted to direct my reaction toward _____

_____

and was tempted to _____

_____ .

What I actually did was _____

_____ ,

which I now understand and take responsibility for, even as I recognize that
a better way of responding would have been _____

_____

_____ .

Learning from this experience, I can now be more mindful and _____

_____

_____ the next time something similar happens.

- How can practicing daily inventories help you address your character defects
  and take responsibility for your actions? How can practicing spot-check inventories, both mentally and in writing, produce greater serenity and peace in your life?

- What concerns do you have about committing to practice daily inventories as
  you work through Step Ten? What aspect seems especially challenging? Why?

- Look back at the fill-in-the-blanks exercise above. What do you now notice about yourself that surprises you? How can you make mental spot-check inventories your go-to when something or someone triggers you?

CONNECTING WITH OTHERS

For you to continue improving in the way you connect with others, you need to persevere in connecting with yourself. Daily inventories facilitate this and become a way for you to remain present with yourself and consciously choose how you respond rather than reacting without regard for consequences. In addition to mental and written daily Spot-Check Inventories, *The Big Book* also suggests you practice a nightly review of how your day went, what you learned, where you succeeded, where you need to improve, what goals you should set for the next day, and, if necessary, what plans you should take to make amends.

In a perfect world, you would immediately notice every time you mess up. You would take steps to prevent it or take care of it right then. But you can't do this perfectly—no one can! Instead, you can be a diligent student of yourself and a spiritual seeker. Practicing a Nightly Inventory helps you in both endeavors.

Like so many other aspects of working the Twelve Steps, there is no single "right" way in doing this inventory. (This has resulted in the creation of a multitude of various tools, approaches, worksheets, inventories, apps, and methods for doing this.) The key is to explore and find what works the best for *you* and how to make it work as effectively as possible for your needs, personality, and lifestyle. You will find the Nightly Inventory that I regularly use in appendix H. I encourage you to give it a try while also searching online, asking your sponsor, listening at meetings, and trying your own approaches.

Lifelong learning is often a crash course. To find balance and maintain peace, you must be willing to adapt, learn as you go, and practice frequent reflective study sessions. Working Step Ten diligently helps you to accept and work with the ways that life meets you where you are right now. Personal inventories assist you with staying on your spiritual journey and learning how to remain on course in the midst of unexpected storms, roadblocks, detours, and debris. Remember, though, that your goal is *progress* in the process. As Bill W. wrote, "For the wise have always known that no one can make much of his life until self-searching has become a regular habit, until he is able to admit and accept what he finds, and until he patiently and persistently tries to correct what is wrong."[8]

- How can practicing daily and nightly inventories benefit your relationships with those closest to you? How has working through Step Ten helped you align with your authentic best self?

- How can regular personal inventories help you avoid accumulations of anger, resentment, and self-hatred? How can these inventories assist you in eliminating procrastination and dealing with issues promptly?

- One of the unexpected challenges of working Step Ten is uncovering more character defects and shortcomings. How can you embrace this possibility as a means to growth and greater peace? How has your attitude toward your character defects shifted since you started working the Steps?

For the next session: Read or review chapter 11, "So Help Me God," in *The Fix*. If you're participating in a group study, plan to share one inventory, awareness tool, or spiritual practice that has helped you to persevere in recovery as you have worked through the Twelve Steps.

11

SEEK HIGHER CONTACT

STEP ELEVEN: Sought through prayer and meditation to improve our conscious contact with God as we understood Him, praying only for knowledge of His will for us and the power to carry that out.

Perhaps you've heard the adage that "you can't step into the same river twice," which dates back to the ancient Greeks and is usually attributed to Heraclitus. The truth of this observation emerges in the reality that change is inevitable. By the time you return to the river a second time, it's no longer the same river because the current has changed, rain or sun has affected the water level, and it's not even the same water. But you've also changed too.

Step Eleven is a reminder that your relationship with God, as you understand and experience him, is similarly changing. While you surrendered to this Greater Power back in Steps Two and Three, by this stage you're ready to be more intentional about your spiritual growth. By now, you've realized that God as you knew him before starting the Twelve Steps (or "the God of my misunderstanding," as one friend in recovery likes to say) was obscured by all kinds of personal baggage, past experiences, and possibly religious trauma. The Steps invited you to reconsider who God is and hit reset on how you relate to him.

In order to reach Step Eleven, you've learned to relinquish control and rely on your Higher Power for strength, courage, and power to persevere beyond your human limits. You've realized that God is not out to get you, condemn you, punish you, mock you, or ignore you. The God you're getting to know is rather an unexpectedly kind, generous, tender, fierce, gracious, and loving spiritual Force.

This God is not only for you but is also intent on helping you experience freedom from your addictions in ways you cannot make happen on your own.

Bill Wilson believed prayer and meditation were the practices best suited to help us make conscious contact with God and grow in our newfound spirituality. While the truth of this is supported by tons of historical, scientific, personal, psychological, and neurological evidence, most of us have the same kinds of biases about prayer and meditation that we used to have about God.

Perhaps you associate prayer and meditation with religious legalism, boring traditionalism, or theological dogmatism. You may have learned to pray (and meditate) in ways that seemed rigid, impersonal, irrelevant, or ridiculous. Whatever your experience, I hope by now you realize that this spiritual journey you've traversing is not bound by any denomination, religious tradition, church, or group. There is a wealth of spiritual practices from countless (and often surprising) sources that you will find helpful as you explore and grow in your faith. I've shared most of mine in chapter 11 of *The Fix*. You will also find a few sample prayers and meditations, including one for centering prayer, in appendix I at the end of this workbook.

The key to working Step Eleven is to recognize and set aside your biases based on past experiences. Just as you have discovered a fresh and uniquely personal dynamic for relating to God as you understand him, you can try different ways to relate, connect, and communicate with him as you proceed to evolve and grow spiritually. Step Eleven, being one of the maintenance steps, directs your attention to maintaining your dependence on your Greater Power. Even better, it invites you to be surprised by the many ways that you can experience divine presence, power, and purpose in your life.

* How has your understanding of God or your Higher Power changed since you began working the Twelve Steps? What previous misconceptions, biases, and false assumptions used to obscure your understanding of God?

- As you've grown spiritually by surrendering to God and relying on his power, how has your understanding of "God's will" changed or evolved? What spiritual concerns, fears, and doubts linger as you seek God's will for your life?

- How does your ego continue to try and impede your relationship with God? What sneaky tactics and default patterns does your ego use to avoid trusting God?

- What daily practices, habits, and reminders have you found helpful in keeping you close to God? Which ones work the best for you and your lifestyle? Which ones aren't as effective or feasible for you right now?

MEETING YOU WHERE YOU ARE

Your recovery journey in working the Twelve Steps has initiated healing in how you relate to God, yourself, and others. In these maintenance steps, you're learning to pedal forward spiritually on your own without relying on training wheels. You still need God and other people, as well as self-awareness, self-compassion, and self-forgiveness. If you veer from the work you've been doing in hopes of coasting, then you will miss the rich benefits offered by Step Eleven.

If you only skim the surface of this eleventh Step, then you will end up reverting to your own efforts and ego-fueled willpower. No matter how much you've grown or changed, you will never outgrow the basic premise stated in Step One: *You're powerless and your life is a mess without God.* You simply cannot overcome your addictions and self-defeating behaviors, grow spiritually, or experience true serenity according to your own terms and unaided efforts. If you try, then you're just setting yourself up for failure and the discouragement and disappointment that comes with it. Or, worse, you will just be propping up your sneaky, relentless ego by clothing yourself in self-righteousness and false piety. For the love of the God of your understanding, don't do it!

Discovering new ways to experience and communicate with your Higher Power is more than worth the effort of exploration and experimentation. While there are many ways to pray and meditate, the best methods for you will quiet and soothe your raucous ego as you serenely align with God's will for your life—no matter what his will might entail. Yes, it's scary to "let go and let God," as so many longtime Twelve Steps walkers urge us, but the joy of discovering connection and union with him and his purposes transcends our fears and doubts.

The joy of divine connection doesn't mean you're never afraid or never have doubts. It simply means you're willing to trust God a little bit more than you used to trust him. It means you're going to follow him even when it doesn't make sense and that you want what he offers more than anything you can attain on your own. This mindset will enable you to focus on surrendering not just once or twice in the first three Steps but again and again every day. The one prayer Bill W. repeatedly emphasizes for recovery is, "Thy will be done."[9]

Praying for God's will to be done and living into it as he reveals his plan requires ongoing self-surrender and radical faith. Remaining openhanded on a daily basis so you can truly accept life on life's terms relies on courage, discipline, and diligence. There's no way to sustain what you need without continuing to rely on how you got this far. Step Eleven invites you to open up new channels for divine connectivity, which in turn results in greater freedom to enjoy peace, balance, and wholeness.

* What is your understanding of God's will for your life at this stage in your recovery journey? What is the basis for this understanding?

- When do you seem to struggle to experience a spiritual connection with God? What prevents or distracts you from seeking his guidance during these struggles?

- How did you learn to pray the way you presently pray? What changes in the way you pray would make it easier for you to talk with God?

- How frequently do you pray for *God's* will to be done as compared to asking for *your* will be done? How can you express your personal hopes and desires while also yielding to God's will?

MOVING FORWARD

Just as there's no one right way to work the Steps, there's no definite way to pray and meditate. The key is to focus on discovering what methods work the best for you. By the time you've reached Step Eleven, you've grown in self-awareness and learned to discern the internal urges of your ego compared to your Inner Observer. You're probably eager to connect with God in ways that allow you to experience more of who he really is and not who you once assumed he was.

Nonetheless, I encourage you to approach prayer and meditation intentionally, which means with a plan that addresses the details. You may have some idea already what works for you and what doesn't based on past experience. Use this knowledge, but also be willing to try some of the old methods that might surprise you. After all, you've changed. What if it wasn't the way you were praying or the particular prayer content stifling you spiritually but your own attitude, ego, and addictions? Bottom line, don't be afraid to reconsider some traditional approaches to prayer along with familiar prayers and scriptural passages.

For prayer and meditation to work, you need consistent communication, as any relationship requires. If you wait until you're struggling, desperate, or tempted to relapse, it's usually too late. Instead of relying on prayer as a last resort, cultivate your connection with God in ways that make prayer a natural first response. In fact, you can converse with God whenever, wherever, and however you want. Rather than having to be on your knees or sitting in a church pew, you can (and should) practice praying and experiencing God's presence no matter what you're doing. It's about cultivating a mindset, an openness, an awareness, and a seeking heart that's plugged in to God as part of your everyday life—not something descending from the heavenlies above.

In terms of what you pray, don't be shy about trying out the prayers of others. Whether these are psalms found in the Old Testament or something your sponsor just texted you last night, remain open to different forms and various expressions for communing with God. I'm a bit of a traditionalist with a twist. I draw on time-tested prayers found in the Bible, *The Big Book*, and *The Book of Common Prayer*, but I also remain open to other faith traditions, fiction and poetry, and contemporary music genres.

I also like to include meditation as part of my daily spiritual practice. While you might associate meditation as an Eastern tradition, or one that's New Age and free-form, it actually has a long and storied history in the Christian tradition. It invites you to connect with God in a way that's similar yet slightly distinct from traditional prayer. One form that combines the best of both, at least as I see it, is called centering prayer (for more info check out appendix I). This practice ushers you into God's presence as you silently surrender your heart and mind to him. You're not required to use words or think, feel, or say anything. You simply pursue connecting with God at a spiritual level.

I find that mornings are the best time for me to pray because it sets the tone for the rest of the day and anchors my awareness of myself to a greater awareness of God. My morning prayer time includes the same elements and usually follows the same pattern. My time in prayer draws on Scripture-based prayers, spiritual readings, journaling, recovery prayers, spontaneous prayer, and silent meditation or centering prayers. While that might sound like it requires half my day, it typically runs around half an hour.

Step Eleven gives you license to pick and choose the practices and sources that work the best for you. Which is why it's important to continue trying out other ways even when you feel comfortable with what you've found effective. Throughout the process, though, don't lose sight of your goals as stated in Step Eleven: (1) conscious contact with God, (2) knowledge of his will for your life, and (3) the power necessary to carry out his will for your life. Prayer and meditation provide the means to persevere in the Steps as you become more of who God created you to be—a beloved human being bearing his divine image.

- What are some ways and models of prayer and meditation that have *not* worked well for you in the past? Which ones are you willing to reconsider and try again?

- What associations or experiences do you have with meditation? What assumptions or preconceived notions do you need to release in order to try meditation or centering prayer as part of your daily spiritual practice?

- How can you incorporate music, visual art, culinary experiences, and natural beauty into the ways you pray and experience God? What are some examples of these unexpected ways you've encountered and enjoyed God's presence?

- Think about which faith traditions and spiritual practices you would like to use to experience greater contact with God (as you understand him). Choose at least three methods or practices (and I highly recommend centering prayer) to try as part of your regular time of connecting with God. List these choices below.

    1. _____

    2. _____

    3. _____

- Here are the components that I use each morning during my time of prayer and meditation. Put a check next to any that you are already practicing. Place a star next to any that you would like to pursue or explore in more detail. Mark an X beside any that don't appeal to you right now or that haven't worked for you in the past. Finally, add your own models, sources, or methods that you want to include as foundational in your prayer and meditation practices.

    ___ Opening prayer or psalm
    ___ Reading a passage of Scripture
    ___ Writing in a gratitude journal
    ___ 15 minutes of silent meditation
    ___ Prayers for others (petitions)
    ___ "Deliver me" prayers (supplication)
    ___ Closing prayer (benediction)
    ___ Other models, sources, or methods you want to include:

CONNECTING WITH OTHERS

Like other aspects of your recovery journey, your experiences with prayer will likely ebb and flow. Sometimes your circumstances will make it challenging for you to pray, but know that these times are often when you will experience the most benefit—whether you feel it at the time or not. You may often find yourself wondering if your prayer and meditation practices really make any difference. That's okay. Feel free to wonder, but then quickly ask your Inner Observer, your Higher Power, and a trusted friend or sponsor for reassurance that your prayers and meditations do indeed make a significant difference.

After you've been praying and meditating for a while, you will more frequently begin to glimpse God at work in your life and the lives of others. One day you may suddenly realize you're doing things you've been trying to do all your life but have failed to accomplish on your own. Celebrate these epiphanies—give thanks and put them at the top of that day's gratitude list! Over time, you will gradually feel more grounded and centered in God throughout the day, regardless of its ups and downs. You will become more cognizant of your Inner Observer, and your ability and willingness to take a pause in the heat of a hard moment will strengthen. You will be more patient with others, you won't easily take offense, and you will become more loving, compassionate, generous, and tolerant with yourself and with those around you.

Your awareness and perceptive appreciation for life will intensify, and you will rediscover feelings of awe and wonder. Laughter will come easier, especially laughing at yourself and your mistakes, and you will carry gratitude for the most mundane moments. You will notice you're no longer focused on what used to appeal to you but instead feel more alive and present than ever before. You will wonder how this happened and then smile as you recognize the way prayer and meditation has allowed God to change you from the inside out.

You're not there yet, but you're moving in a divine direction as you connect with God and seek the power to do his will. The result is sober serenity, emotional equilibrium, and a stronger faith in your Higher Power and his love for you.

- When have your most recently experienced close connection with your Higher Power and a clearer understanding of his will for your life? What means and methods helped facilitate your connection and understanding?

- How has working Step Eleven changed the way you view prayer and meditation? How do you see them differently now than you did before working the Steps?

- How do you respond to the wording of Step Eleven to pray "only" for knowledge of God's will and the power to carry it out? How does your understanding of "only" affect the way you pray or consciously connect with God?

- How do trusted others help you gain knowledge and understanding of God's will for your life? What's an example of how someone has helped you with this in the past week?

For the next session: Read or review chapter 12, "It Works If You Work It," along with the final Epilogue in *The Fix*. If you're participating in a group study, choose one way you've experienced God through the other members of your group that you're willing to share.

12

SHARE WITH OTHERS

Step Twelve: Having had a spiritual awakening as the result of these Steps, we tried to carry this message [to our fellow sufferers], and to practice these principles in all our affairs.

You've probably encountered those books that say something like, "Everything I needed to know about life, I learned from _____ " (Kindergarten, *Peanuts, Sesame Street, Buffy, The Sopranos,* Harry Potter, Baby Yoda—you get the idea). But for my money, there's no better teacher for what matters most in life and how to experience it than the Twelve Steps.

Without a doubt, we would all be better off—as individuals and every collective group up to a global level—if we had been taught and implemented the Twelve Steps as preschoolers. They are the directions for living that we've had to learn the hard way—but have grown to appreciate as the lifesaving principles they are. The Twelve Steps are as simple as they are profound. We learn to make peace with God, ourselves, and others and cultivate a lifestyle that supports health and growth in each of those important domains.

But Step Twelve takes it one step further (no pun intended, I promise!). Reaching the "dozen" milestone Step instructs you with one last gold nugget for refining yourself and experiencing all the fullness of life: *You can't keep it if you don't give away what you've learned.*

In many ways, Step Twelve is the culmination of all the progress you've made working the other Steps. Keep in mind the purpose of the Twelve Steps is to facilitate a spiritual awakening that not only transforms your personality (the way you act, think, feel, and view the world), and not only trades your need for an addictive substance or behavior for a spiritual awakening, but also leaves the world a better place than you found it. Diligently working the Twelve Steps will empower you to manage the inescapable pain of life without relying on substances and behaviors that numb, distract, and destroy you.

Step Twelve reveals that the process you are experiencing while working the Steps is similar to what countless others have experienced—while also remaining uniquely your own. The more you're around others on a similar recovery journey, the more you also realize there are as many different kinds of spiritual awakenings as there are people who have them. While some people have sudden and dramatic spiritual experiences, you shouldn't expect that to be your experience or despair if it takes longer than you want or expect. Most people will tell you their spiritual awakenings happened gradually as they progressed through the Steps. I suspect that most spiritual awakenings are so subtle and incremental that other people will often notice the changes in you before you do.

Step Twelve brings you full circle, making it clear that for you to continue to grow and flourish, you must serve others by sharing your story and what you've learned so far on your journey of recovery.

• What have you learned about being a better person from working the Steps? What are a couple ways you've experienced a richer life from doing the Steps?

• What's the single greatest benefit of working the Steps right now? How do they equip and empower you to face the hardest challenges in your life?

- What are two or three pieces of wisdom about working the Twelve Steps that you've gleaned from others on a similar journey? How have you benefited from the efforts of others who are also working through Step Twelve?

- How do you know that the changes in your life result from your spiritual awakening and the power of God at work in your life? What evidence do you see that the ways you're changing could never take place without divine involvement?

MEETING YOU WHERE YOU ARE

If you want to see how far you've come on your spiritual journey of recovery, one reliable indicator is to consider the size of your ego. As you begin to shift your primary preoccupation from self-preservation to others-based service, you will notice that your previous center of the universe—yourself!—has moved at least a few degrees beyond your own prior interests. You no longer think only of what benefits *you* every time. You're willing to consider the burdens that others are carrying and not just your own. You realize new levels of patience, humility, and compassion springing from inside you.

Bill Wilson considered self-centeredness to be the root of our troubles. He knew that an untamed ego is an overinflated, insecure, defensive hub for fear-based and anger-fueled self-absorption. The human ego always wants to be the center of attention—even when hiding in addictions and compulsive behaviors. The ego constantly compares itself to others and craves external validation. It's committed to self-protection and self-promotion, always desperately hiding in the nearest spotlight.

When you continue to surrender to your Higher Power, you will gradually realize that a transformation has been taking place within you. You begin to think of yourself *less* because you're focused on others *more*. This shift is so supernatural that there's no way you can begin to take credit for it. It's simply what happens when you surrender yourself to God, face the hard truths about yourself, make peace with others, and commit to a spiritual path that compassionately monitors and right-sizes your ego. In other words—when you work the Steps.

Please understand this transformation has nothing to do with thinking less of yourself or becoming a martyr who serves everyone out of a punitive attempt to sublimate their egocentricity. No, working the Twelve Steps makes it clear that you've invited God into the process of living moment by moment, hour by hour, day by day. You've embraced the fact that in order to meet life on life's terms, you need help—and a lot of it. You no longer feel compelled to try and white-knuckle your way through the painful realities of life because you realize you're not alone—others are alongside you to support, encourage, and truth-check. Best of all, you're awake to the immense beauty and serenity of deepening your relationship with God, a loving Higher Power you can actually trust.

Somewhere along the way, your ego lost control of the wheel and charting your course. You've now learned to make peace with your ego and recognize its wily ways without shaming it or villainizing it. You're at peace because you no longer have anything to prove or disprove. You have tasted divine love and realize you're connected to a limitless source who's committed to loving you despite your best attempts to sabotage your surrender to such unconditional favor. You're wide awake spiritually and eager to sound the alarm for others who continue to sleep on the job. Which is what Step Twelve is all about!

- How have you experienced your ego's preoccupation with yourself diminish while working through the Twelve Steps? What evidence do you see that you no longer consider yourself the center of the universe?

- What changes in you have those closest to you observed or commented on since you've been on this journey of Step-based recovery? What have they seen that escaped your notice?

- What no longer upsets you or triggers fear, anger, and resentment like it used to ignite in you? When was the last time you noticed that you no longer reacted to stressors the way you once did?

- How could sharing your experiences with "fellow sufferers" benefit them? How could it benefit you as well?

MOVING FORWARD

Working the Twelve Steps results in a full life makeover. Each Step contributes to a new way of thinking, feeling, processing, understanding, choosing, and acting. While there's a lot of overlap, each Step builds on the work completed with previous Steps, strengthening your spiritual muscles through the process. Rather than resigning yourself to a descent into the madness of futility, you now experience freedom from your self-imposed shackles of addiction. How? It all began with the foundation laid by Step One, which established the primary principle of complete *honesty*. From there, each subsequent Step offered you a new spiritual ingredient for living in freedom. Let's recap some of these.

Step Two invited you to embrace the spiritual principle of *hope*. Fueled by hope, you began trusting in your Greater Power and taking baby steps toward the love and power that was available to you.

Step Three facilitated the principle of *faith*—believing that no matter what happens, God has you. Even when you can't imagine how everything will be okay, you believe by faith that love is greater than fear.

Step Four instilled you with *courage*. Working through this fourth Step, you discovered the strength to stare down your shadow and accept the hard truths about yourself on a regular basis.

Step Five promoted the principle of *integrity*. You realized you can now align your values and beliefs with the rest of you, closing the gap between what you say you care about and what you do that shows your true priorities.

Step Six emphasized the essential spiritual principle of *willingness*. You realized you're not in control of how life unfolds but that you remain responsible for your choices and actions.

Step Seven encapsulated the principle of *humility*, instructing you on how to move beyond your prideful ego in order to live freely in serenity.

Step Eight facilitated the practice of *forgiveness*. You realized that forgiving others and yourself enabled you to ask others to forgive you.

Step Nine followed through on reconciliation with those you've hurt, showing them the power of *love* in action.

Step Ten kept on keeping on through the principle of *perseverance*, giving you inventories and other tools to practice your new principles on a daily basis.

Step Eleven taught you *spiritual wakefulness*, or the process of increasing your God-consciousness. As you grow more in love with Divine Love, you become more willing to trust God's will for your life.

Step Twelve showed you that the process was never about stopping your addictions but about starting to live fully and freely. Liberated and empowered, you now live according to the spiritual principle of *service*.

Living the Twelve Steps teaches you how to keep going no matter what life throws at you. You realize that resisting your addictions and self-destructive behaviors is only the beginning of your spiritual adventure. The Steps equip you to be a healthy adult. You suit up, show up, and grow up. The process will always be tricky and sometimes painful, which is why you take it one day at a time. You meet life on life's terms but with a spiritual perspective and divine demeanor that elevates you above it. Working the Twelve Steps allows you to give back what you've been given. You experience the joy that comes from being a conduit of grace as you bless others with the blessings you've received on your journey.

- Which spiritual principles and gifts have made the biggest difference in your recovery journey so far? How have those specific principles and gifts helped you to move forward in your spiritual awakening?

- Which of the Twelve Steps have been especially challenging to work through? What have you learned by persevering through the requirements of each Step?

- What would you tell someone who is just beginning their journey of working the Twelve Steps? If you were asked to be a sponsor for a newbie to recovery, what one suggestion or recommendation would you offer?

- Which of the Steps do you know you want to work again now that you've been through all twelve? How will you work it differently this next time?

CONNECTING WITH OTHERS

"Use it or lose it," said a friend in recovery upon learning I had reached Step Twelve. I smiled at her pithy response but knew the profound truth of what she was conveying. And now I impart the same message to you.

If you don't regularly draw on your newfound recovery and share the miracle of what you've experienced with others, you'll soon regress. Your ego will see an opportunity to take credit for your transformation, and before you know it, your spiritual muscles will grow flabby and atrophy. Giving back and serving others lets you flex your newly developed spirituality without making it about you.

Nonetheless, there's nothing wrong with recognizing the benefits you receive from sharing what you've been given with others on a similar journey. The only way to keep what you have is to give it away. Bill W. wrote, "Practical experience shows that nothing will so much insure immunity from drinking [or any other addiction] as intensive work with other alcoholics [addicts]."[10] So true!

The way you serve others can take many forms. Obviously, if you're a member of a Twelve Step recovery community (like Alcoholics Anonymous, Overeaters Anonymous, Gamblers Anonymous, Sex and Love Addicts Anonymous), you can serve newcomers by carpooling to meetings, becoming a sponsor, setting up the meeting room, and welcoming people as they arrive. You can also serve them by listening and offering words of encouragement when they need it or sharing your own recovery story with someone who asks to hear it.

Serving others, however, extends far beyond regular meetings and check-ins. You will be surprised at the opportunities to serve that open up when you're willing to help others. So remain vigilant for ways to love and serve others everywhere you go—at home, at the office, or whenever the opportunity arises. You never know how God will use you to awaken someone else.

- What do you know about the Twelve Steps now that you didn't know when you began working Step One? How has your perspective on working the Steps changed in light of reaching Step Twelve?

- What are a couple of the big takeaways that will stay with you now that you've completed this workbook and finished reading *The Fix*? What difference will this experience have in the way you live your life on a daily basis?

- Who have you already been serving and helping on their own Step journey of recovery? What have you discovered you have to offer that surprises you?

- What's one new way you want to be of service to others on a similar journey in the weeks to come? What action do you need to take today in order to get started?

RESENTMENT INVENTORY

Person I hold a resentment toward	What this person did to me	How this behavior affected me	What role I played in this episode
Example: my mother	She was controlling and critical	It made me feel ashamed and like I was never good enough	I was an unruly kid who was hard to handle

FEAR INVENTORY

People, places, principles, institutions, ideas, and things that cause me to fear	How my fear of these things has affected me
Example: I'm afraid of disappointing people	My fear of disappointing people has led to my saying yes to things I don't want to do and beoming resentful toward others

SEXUAL CONDUCT INVENTORY

Whom did I harm sexually?	What was the cause of my sexual conduct?	What should I have done instead?
Example: my ex-girlfriend (ex-boyfriend)	I was selfishly seeking validation and proof that our relationship was solid	I should have shared my insecurities and asked for reassurance

GENERAL HARMS DONE INVENTORY

Whom did I harm?	What was the cause of my conduct?	What should I have done instead?
Example: I abruptly broke up with my partner without explanation	Fear of conflict	I should have sat down with the person and explained my rationale for breaking up

SKELETONS IN THE CLOSET INVENTORY

What secret am I keeping that I don't want anyone else to know about?	How does keeping this secret impact my life?
Example: I was sexually abused when I was 10	The memory of this experience makes me feel ashamed and unworthy of love

APPENDIX F

LETTER TO FIFTH STEP LISTENER

Dear [listener's name],

[Your name] has asked you to participate with [him/her] in a journey [he/she] has been going through in the Twelve Steps. As part of this process, [your name] would like to share a set of personal inventories that [he/she] has recorded of [his/her] past resentments, fears, mistaken beliefs, and misconducts. Here are some basic instructions on how to participate with [your name] in this Step in the event that you have not done this before.

First, know that your primary role will be to support [your name] and not judge or criticize [him/her]. This will enable [your name] to have a place where [he/she] can openly and honestly share [his/her] deepest thoughts and feelings with you without fear or shame. Try to really listen to [your name] as these inventories are being shared and avoid interrupting [him/her]. Ask questions if you need clarification on something that is said, but keep the fact that [your name] is being vulnerable in sharing this information with you at the forefront of your mind.

Here are a few other important points to keep in mind as a listener:

- *Keep everything you hear to yourself and don't share it with others.*
- *Maintain eye contact and use nonverbal cues (like nodding) to show that you are engaged and fully paying attention to what [your name] is saying.*
- *If you need to ask any questions for clarification, keep them open-ended and avoid pressuring [your name] to disclose more than [he/she] is ready to share.*
- *Resist the urge to offer solutions, give advice, or try to fix the problems.*
- *Be aware of your reactions. Do not respond with shock, disbelief, or judgment. Ask to take a minute pause if you need time to process something that is said.*

- *Try to validate [your name]'s feelings and show you are empathetic toward [his/her] struggles. Let [your name] know that you are there for [him/her].*

When [your name] is finished sharing, express your appreciation that [he/she] has trusted you enough to be willing to share [his/her] story. Encourage [your name] to persevere through the Twelve Steps. Finally, if appropriate, talk about ways you can continue to support [him/her].

Thank you for your willingness to be an active listener! You are playing a vital role in helping [your name] stay the course on [his/her] journey of recovery.

APPENDIX G

LIST OF CHARACTER DEFECTS

Aimless	Ambitious (overly)	Analytical (overly)	Angry
Apprehensive	Anxious	Autocratic (overly)	Apathetic
Avoiding	Blocking	Closed-minded	Careless
Codependent	Combative	Condescending	Conceited
Contrary	Conflict-avoidant	Contemptuous	Controlling
Cowardly	Cynical	Deceitful	Defensive
Depressed	Dependent (overly)	Detached	Discourteous
Dishonest	Disloyal	Disobedient	Disrespectful
Distant	Distracted	Distrusting	Dogmatic
Domineering	Dualistic-thinking	Enabling	Entitled
Envious	Excessive	Faithless	Fearful
Forgetful	Gaslighting	Gluttonous	Gossiping
Greedy	Guilty	Hypercritical	Hypersensitive
Idealistic (overly)	Ill-tempered	Immature	Immodest
Impatient	Inconsiderate	Indecisive	Indulgent (overly)
Inflexible	Inferior (complex)	Insecure	Insincere
Intolerant	Intellectual (snobbery)	Irresponsible	Isolated
Jealous	Judgmental	Lazy	Legalistic
Lustful	Manipulative	Martyrdom-prone	Masking
Melancholic	Miserly	Misunderstood	Moody
Narcissistic	Narrow-minded	Negative	Neglectful
Obsessive	Numb (emotionally)	Obstructive	Paranoid
Patronizing	Passive-aggressive	People-pleasing	Perfectionistic
Pessimistic	Possessive	Posturing-prone	Preachy
Prejudiced	Procrastinative	Proud	Reckless
Resentful	Rigid	Rude	Sarcastic

Self-centered	Self-deceitful	Self-defeating	Self-hating
Self-justifying	Self-neglectful	Self-pitying	Self-promoting
Self-righteous	Self-seeking	Shameful	Short-sighted
Shy	Spiteful	Stubborn	Sullen
Superstitious	Suspicious	Tense	Thrill-seeking
Treacherous	Unavailable	Undisciplined	Unempathetic
Unforgiving	Unfriendly	Ungrateful	Unrealistic
Unworthy	Vain	Vengeful	Verbose
Vindictive	Violent	Vulgar	Wasteful
Willful	Withdrawn	Workaholic-prone	Worried

APPENDIX H
NIGHTLY INVENTORY

1. Was I resentful?

2. Was I dishonest?

3. Did I promptly admit when I was wrong?

4. Do I owe anyone an apology or amends?

5. Did I do or say something out of fear?

6. Have I kept something to myself that should be discussed with another person immediately?

7. Did I think today of what I could do for others?

8. Was I kind and loving toward all?

9. Did I reach out to someone in recovery today to ask how they were doing?

10. What could I have done better?

APPENDIX I

PRAYERS AND MEDITATIONS

As mentioned in Step Eleven, there is a wealth of spiritual practices from many sources that you will find helpful as you explore and grow in your faith. I've shared most of mine in chapter 11 of *The Fix*, but here are a few additional prayers and meditations that you might want to try.

CENTERING PRAYER

One type of prayer that I definitely recommend is *centering prayer*, which is based on Jesus' words in Matthew 6:6: "When you pray, go into your room, close the door and pray to your Father, who is unseen. Then your Father, who sees what is done in secret, will reward you." Centering prayer ushers you into God's presence as you surrender your heart and mind to him. Here is the basic technique for centering prayer that I outlined in *The Fix:*

1. **Choose a sacred word**. This word isn't a mantra but an anchor you'll repeatedly return to and focus on when you catch yourself reengaging with your thoughts. Your sacred word could be *Jesus, love, present,* or, my go-to—*shalom*. Some people use an abbreviated form of the Jesus Prayer: "Lord, have mercy on me." Once you've chosen your word or short phrase, stick with it.

2. **Say your sacred word.** Sit in a comfortable position with your eyes closed, relax, and silently say your sacred word as "the symbol of your consent to God's presence and action within."

3. **Repeat your sacred word.** When your attention wanders (and it will), gently return to your sacred word until your mind quiets again.

Then, when your mind has calmed and repeating your sacred word is no longer necessary, let it go.

4. **Sit quietly for a time.** When you're finished, sit quietly for a few minutes and enjoy the afterglow of your time in God's presence. Then slowly open your eyes, get up, and fire up the espresso machine.

Here are a few other common sacred words that you could use: *Abba, God, Father, Spirit, faith, grace, holy, mercy, peace, joy, trust, stillness, silence, listen, release, calm, amen.*

SERENITY PRAYER

The following prayer was originally written in the 1930s by Reinhold Niebuhr, a theologian, commentator on politics and public affairs, and professor at Union Theological Seminary in New York. It gained popularity among his colleagues and was widely circulated without reference to him as the author. The prayer was adapted over time until it was published by Niebuhr in a magazine column in 1951, at which point it took on the form that we recognize it today. The second clause was later added in *Origin of the Serenity Prayer: A Historic Paper.*

God, grant me the serenity
to accept the things I cannot change,
the courage to change the things I can,
and the wisdom to know the difference.

Living one day at a time,
enjoying one moment at a time,
accepting hardship as a pathway to peace,
taking, as He did, the sinful world as it is,
not as I would have it,
trusting that He will make all things right,
if I surrender to His will,
that I may be reasonably happy in this life,
and supremely happy with Him forever in the next.[11]

SECOND STEP PRAYER (THE SET ASIDE PRAYER)

This is a famous prayer in Twelve-Step circles that captures the posture you should adopt as you approach Step Two of desiring to have an open mind:

> *God, today help me set aside everything I think I know about you, everything I think I know about myself, everything I think I know about others, and everything I think I know about my own recovery [my own life] so I may have an open mind and a new experience with all these things. Please help me see the truth.*[12]

THE THIRD STEP PRAYER

This is a great prayer from *The Big Book* that you can recite if you're unpracticed with prayer and worried about saying the wrong thing:

> *God, I offer myself to Thee—to build with me and to do with me as Thou wilt. Relieve me of the bondage of self, that I may better do Thy will. Take away my difficulties, that victory over them may bear witness to those I would help of Thy Power, Thy Love, and Thy Way of life. May I do Thy will always!*[13]

THE SEVENTH STEP PRAYER

The first thing I do every morning when I get up is get on my knees and pray this prayer, which is also found in *The Big Book*:

> *My Creator, I am now willing that you should have all of me, good and bad. I pray that you now remove from me every single defect of character which stands in the way of my usefulness to you and my fellows. Grant me strength, as I go out from here to do Your bidding.*[14]

ELEVENTH STEP PRAYER

The following prayer, often used in Twelve Steps groups, is associated with the Italian Saint Francis of Assisi, though it is not found in his writings. The first appearance of the prayer can be traced to a French magazine published in 1912 by a Catholic organization in Paris.

Lord, make me an instrument of thy peace.
Where there is hatred, let me sow love;
Where there is injury, pardon;
Where there is doubt, faith;
Where there is despair, hope;
Where there is darkness, light;
Where there is sadness, joy.
O divine Master, grant that I may not so much seek
To be consoled as to console,
To be understood as to understand,
To be loved as to love;
For it is in giving that we receive;
It is in pardoning that we are pardoned;
It is in dying to self that we are born to eternal life.

THOMAS MERTON PRAYER

Thomas Merton was an American Trappist monk, writer, theologian, poet, social activist and scholar of comparative religion. The following prayer, first published in *Thoughts in Solitude* in 1958, is about reaching outward to God and inward to one's true self.

My Lord God,
I have no idea where I am going.
I do not see the road ahead of me.
I cannot know for certain where it will end.
nor do I really know myself,
and the fact that I think I am following your will
does not mean that I am actually doing so.

But I believe that the desire to please you
does in fact please you.
And I hope I have that desire in all that I am doing.
I hope that I will never do anything apart from that desire.
And I know that if I do this you will lead me by the right road,
though I may know nothing about it.
Therefore will I trust you always though
I may seem to be lost and in the shadow of death.
I will not fear, for you are ever with me,
and you will never leave me to face my perils alone.[15]

NOTES

1. Bill Wilson, *Alcoholics Anonymous: The Story of How Many Thousands of Men and Women Have Recovered from Alcoholism*, 4th ed. (New York: Alcoholics Anonymous World Services, 2001), 46. Also known as *The Big Book,* as referenced in this workbook.
2. Wilson, *Alcoholics Anonymous*, 64.
3. Wilson, *Alcoholics Anonymous*, 68.
4. Richard Attenborough, director, *Shadowlands* (Paramount Pictures, 1993).
5. Wilson, *Alcoholics Anonymous*, 76.
6. Wilson, *Alcoholics Anonymous*, 83–84.
7. Bill Wilson, *Twelve Steps and Twelve Traditions* (New York: Alcoholics Anonymous World Services, Inc., 2001), 90.
8. Wilson, *Twelve Steps and Twelve Traditions*, 88.
9. See Wilson, *Alcoholics Anonymous*, 63, 67, 85, 87–88.
10. Wilson, *Alcoholics Anonymous*, 89
11. Nell Wing, "Origin of the Serenity Prayer: A Historic Paper," Alcoholics Anonymous, Service Material from the General Service Office (pdf), chrome-extension://efaidnb mnnnibpcajpcglclefindmkaj/https://www.aa.org/sites/default/files/literature/assets/smf-129_en.pdf.
12. Paul Greene, "The Set Aside Prayer," Manhattan Center for Cognitive Behavioral Therapy, https://manhattancbt.com/set-aside-prayer.
13. Wilson, *Alcoholics Anonymous*, 63.
14. Wilson, *Alcoholics Anonymous*, 76.
15. Thomas Merton, "The Merton Prayer" from *Thoughts in Solitude* (The Abbey of Our Lady of Gethsemani 1956).

ABOUT THE AUTHOR

Ian Morgan Cron is a bestselling author, psychotherapist, trained spiritual director, Enneagram teacher, and Episcopal priest. As someone who works a Twelve-Steps program, he's a knowledge-able, compassionate, and humorous guide on the road to recov-ery. Ian accepts a limited number of private coaching clients to thoughtfully guide them on their personal and professional path. He and his wife, Anne, live in Nashville, Tennessee. Find out more at **ianmorgancron.com**.